If It's Not One Thing, It's Your Mother

BY THE SAME AUTHOR

God Said, "Ha!"

It's Pat! My Life Exposed

If It's Not One Thing, It's Your Mother

Julia Sweeney

BLOOMSBURY

LONDON · NEW DELHI · NEW YORK · SYDNEY

First published in Great Britain 2013

Copyright © 2013 by Julia Sweeney

The moral right of the author has been asserted

No part of this book may be used or reproduced in any manner whatsoever
without written permission from the Publisher except in the case of brief
quotations embodied in critical articles or reviews

Bloomsbury Publishing Plc
50 Bedford Square
London
WC1B 3DP

www.bloomsbury.com

Bloomsbury Publishing, London, New Delhi, New York and Sydney
A CIP catalogue record for this book is available from the British Library

ISBN 978 1 4088 3063 5
10 9 8 7 6 5 4 3 2 1

Designed by Maura Fadden Rosenthal
Printed and bound in Great Britain by CPI Group (UK) Ltd, Croydon CR0 4YY

For Mulan

And my mom

Through whom

I am enmeshed

In the sticky web

of

Motherhood

Contents

Contents

WEEK THREE ~ Death

WEEK FOUR ~ Dependence

Prologue

I want to be alone. I really need to be alone.

I took so long to assemble my lovely family. I did it all a bit backward: first a delightful daughter, then a beloved husband. I went after creating family, like a golden retriever running after a ball—how much does the dog think about what he's doing? He doesn't think. He does. He is a doer. That's me, too. I did it, I do it. I am doing it.

Every morning I get up and hustle. I'm sure this is true for most mothers. It's true for me, too. This is what I wanted, after all. This was my dream. I'm always on task. I never go up the stairs of our house without looking around for what needs to be taken up. I never buy just one meal's worth of food at the grocery store. I drive the carpools, I volunteer at the school cafeteria. I wait patiently outside the dance classes. I iron. I clean up the cat vomit. Make dinner. Walk the dog. I work (write) at home and then really work, at home. I quell the rising ire in my roommates. I try to instill harmony, efficiency, and a calm, enabling environment for my fellow family members. I often set the table two hours before dinner. I live by lists. I pick up things in our house and put them where they go. Chiefly, I'm the protector against the chaos that threatens us. I am a good soldier.

I love my job.

Secretly I hate my job.

I love my family.

If only they would disappear.

Why do I sometimes find myself entertaining the enticing idea of entering a witness protection program? Why does the desire arise, when I walk my dog to Lake Michigan, to drop the dog leash and swim straight out toward the Upper Peninsula, then on to Montreal, and then over to the Atlantic and into a frothy sea that would suck me into—somehow—incongruously—some calm tranquility?

I just want this family to go away and leave me be.

And now they are leaving me be.

A delightful convergence of circumstances has occurred. My twelve-year-old daughter, Mulan, is going to sleepaway camp, for a month. And my husband, Michael, is going away to work out of town, to Tucson, to Boston, then to Europe, for a month. Well, Michael will be home for three days at the end of the second week, but mostly *I will be here by myself.* People! Can you stand it? I'm so excited. In fact, I'm giddy.

Four weeks by myself. No nudging, no breakfasts, no mad mommy and disgruntled wife. Just me in my house.

I act different when it's just me in my house. I've never gotten four weeks—but I have had a day or two, here and there, to bask in the solitude of my home. A muscle relaxes; the mother/wife/hostess mask slides off. I don't rush around and pick up every little thing. I let the dishes pile up, and the newspapers don't make it to their designated place. I don't make the bed.

Oh. Oh . . . yes. The bed.

I'll get into bed early, around 8:30 P.M. Sometimes even earlier—when it's still light outside. I'll watch TV and let the cat rub up against my feet while I eat ice cream. I'll move all over the bed. It's just there for me. I'll wander around the house and let myself get consumed by a random project. I'll sit on the sofa and listen to the sounds of the street outside. I'll surf the Web in my office for hours. There's going to be no need to look, or even pretend to look, productive.

I have big plans for these four weeks. I want to stay inside. I don't want to go anywhere. Truthfully, this desire has been gathering momentum for a while now. I expected myself to be a careerist, out in the world, living in an urban environment with urbane friends and lots of cocktail parties. But I turned into a woman who doesn't like to leave her house. If I'd known when I was twenty that I was going to turn into the person I am at age fifty-two, I would have cringed. And laughed. No way!

And yet.

That twenty-year-old self knew so little about the delicious taste of solitude.

So come with me; let's spend this month together. If I'm going to be alone, you're coming too, goddamnit. You'll be my compatriot, my conspirator, my secret bearer. I'll tell you my story, and then you'll help me understand. How did I get here? What's that song about finding yourself elsewhere in the world behind the wheel of a large automobile?

Thank you, David Byrne and the Talking Heads, for giving

me—a head who is often talking—the right lyrics. And speaking of large automobiles, mine is a minivan, a Honda Odyssey. An Odyssey! I laughed when I saw it for the first time in Hollywood, realizing I would be driving to the Midwest, and away from my own Trojan war, after having won a certain kind of peace. Some women recoil at the idea of minivans, but not me, not us, not we in the land of minivans.

However, we'll only admire this car from the vantage of the kitchen window, because I'm hoping not to drive for an entire month. And yet, metaphorically speaking, we'll travel near and far. We'll occasionally gaze upon the car, and its existence will figure into a couple of stories. Let it serve us as an icon of our time together. We're going on a journey home, while being at home already.

Perfect.

My favorite kind.

WEEK ONE

Unto Me
a Child
Is Given

CHAPTER ONE

If It's Not One Thing, It's Your Mother

First things first: Let me bring you in the house, which, you may notice, is quite old by American standards. It's located in Wilmette, Illinois. It has a history, this house. It used to be the Village Hall and was originally built in 1878. This house was in existence when the Battle of Little Bighorn was going on, a mere thousand miles to the west. Why this fact is meaningful to me, I'm not exactly sure. But this house—the door frames, the old plaster on the walls of the front rooms, the staircase banister—it links me in time to history, however humbly.

My house sits near the wee town center, which has a train station; in just twenty-eight minutes you can be in downtown Chicago. Michael and I bought this house nearly four years ago, after we married. Mulan and I moved from Los Angeles, moving in with Michael, who was already living a mile from here. We pasted ourselves together and formed a family. When I saw this house for the first time, I had that Brigham Young–like sensation: this is the place. I was in love at first sight, but I pretended to consider other houses, like dating around before you get married to the person you know you'll marry. This house and I were meant for each other. We both knew it. Plus, like Brigham Young, I was really tired and wanted to stop.

The house has been remodeled many times over the years, but the front part of the house is the oldest part. There's a guest room just to the right of the front door. In the guest room we have an antique double bed and we call it the "grandma room." This is because it's often used by Michael's mother, Norma, or my mother, Jeri, when they visit.

On the bed is a decorative pillow. My mother gave this pillow to me about seventeen years ago—when I was single, living in Los Angeles, and not yet a mother. She had come to visit, and as she bent over her suitcase to unpack, she exclaimed, "I brought you the most hysterical thing!" I was a little frightened. Past experience taught me that the object would not, in fact, be hysterical.

Then I watched as she took a small, navy blue pillow out of her suitcase. She was already laughing. The pillow had a phrase embroidered on top: IF IT'S NOT ONE THING, IT'S YOUR MOTHER.

I immediately hated the pillow for two reasons. One was that it was a play on an old catchphrase, "If it's not one thing, it's another." Gilda Radner's character on *Saturday Night Live* Roseanne Roseannadanna used to say that phrase, after she said, "It's always something." The association with *Saturday Night Live* was slightly irritating because I'd just left that very show, and although my departure was on friendly terms I was feeling slightly wounded. However, many people—I think perhaps my mother is included in this group—assumed that as a former cast member I must *love* anything even slightly associated with *SNL*, and I feared that this was part of her assumption when buying that pillow.

The second thing I hated was the rhyming pun (as a rule I do not like those), in which the key word was *mother*, meaning that it was, of course, all about my mother. I thought, the pillow may as well have been embroidered with MY MOTHER IS A FIRST-CLASS NARCISSIST AND ALL I GOT OUT OF IT WAS THIS STUPID PILLOW.

Come to think of it, there was a third reason I hated the pillow, the true objection at the root of it all. It was that the pillow indicated to whoever gazed upon it that my mother and I conversed in a casual yet intimate repartee of mutual ribbing, a jovial "You drive me crazy but I still love you" kind of thing. I felt that my mother and I did not have that kind of relationship.

My mother held the pillow out toward me and I smiled, forcefully.

"Isn't it hysterical?" she asked.

"Yes," I said flatly. "Hysterical."

As soon as my mother left town I put the pillow into a closet.

It only emerged when she came for a visit; I'd prop it up on the guest room bed ahead of her arrival. A few years and several visits went by. One spring, my mother came to visit. She looked affectionately at the pillow. "That pillow is really just so funny," she said. Then she glanced at me, encouraging me to agree.

"Eh . . . ," I said.

"Oh," my mother replied, stung by my lack of enthusiasm. "Well, if you don't like it, get rid of it." She picked up the pillow and pressed it against her breast. Her head looked like a flower emerging from the square shape, her neck and face tilted slightly to one side. A tablespoon of liquid guilt dripped into my lower abdomen.

"No, *I sort of* like it," I meekly offered.

"Oh good!" My mother sighed, relieved.

Years went by. I became a mother myself. The guest room in L.A. became my daughter's room, and the closet where the pillow was kept became my daughter's closet. One day, when Mulan was about four years old, I was cleaning out her closet and I came upon the pillow.

Suddenly, without warning, a flood of emotion came over me. I realized with a start that this pillow really *was* hysterical. I laughed out loud and thought, This pillow needs to be on my daughter's bed. Anyone who walks in is going to laugh.

With a thud, I understood that I'd been much, much too hard on my mother. She wasn't a narcissist! We really did have a casual intimacy that included mutual ribbing. Just like I did, and would continue to have, with my own daughter as she grew older. Of course!

So the pillow's new home was on Mulan's bed. And I was

right: anyone who came over and toured around the house laughed when they saw it. "Where did you get that?" they would ask. "My mother!" I would say. We would both giggle. See, the humor would escalate.

My daughter grew and years passed. When Mulan was six she came to me with the pillow.

"I don't want this on my bed anymore," she said.

"Why?" I asked, adding, "It's hysterical."

"No," Mulan said. "It's not. I don't even get it."

I said, "Well, it's a play on the phrase 'If it's not one thing, it's another.' Like if many bad things are happening to you, or like if one bad thing goes away in your life and then another one pops up."

"That's terrible," Mulan said.

"Yes," I said. "So this pillow takes that phrase, and substitutes the word *mother* for *another*. Like your 'mother' is *another* bad thing that happens to you."

It dawned on me that I was clearly not a bad thing happening to her. At least not yet; I mean, she was only six. In a way, her not getting the joke was a compliment.

Mulan said, "I just don't like it. I don't mean to hurt your feelings, but it's not funny to me. I don't want this pillow in my room." Then she added this, just to twist the knife a little: "You wouldn't want me to have something I really didn't *like* in my room, would you?"

I say "twist the knife" because one thing I want my daughter to be is able to defy and be independent of me, her mother; unlike me, who cowers and does whatever my mother says or wants most of the time. I suppose I have succeeded in cultivating this quality in Mulan, as she has it in spades, and she emphasizes her independence and different opinions constantly. I have vowed to gulp and bear it.

At this point, Mulan sighed wearily at me, indicating that in fact, I was not a totally good thing in her life. Which made me think, "Well, if that was true, why wasn't that pillow funny?"

Then, I realized: clearly the funniness of this pillow does not become apparent until one actually becomes a mother, and the pillow, resting on one's offspring's chair or bed, demonstrates its comic value to all.

My mission was suddenly clear and straightforward: I had to keep this pillow until Mulan did, in fact, think it was funny. That would only occur if Mulan became a mother herself. The pillow went back in the closet.

Through several dramatic reductions of clutter and even a marriage and a move across country, I've held on to that pillow. I think of the pillow now like an insect, the cicada. Here, in the Midwest, there is a species of cicada whose larvae live underground. Depending on the species, they bide their time for thirteen to seventeen years. Then they metamorphose as flying adults into the light of day. I feel the pillow is like the cicada—just biding its time, waiting to be funny again.

But then, a little over a year ago, here in Illinois, I came across the pillow in a basement closet and moved it to the guest room bed. The grandmothers come and go, and the guest room is often empty. But the pillow has found a home in this room.

At this very moment our dog, Arden, is draped over the pillow on the bed. He's an Australian cattle hound, about fifty pounds. His paws cradle the pillow and under his bloodshot eyes you can just read the word *mother*. It's hard not to sigh and linger in the doorway when he looks at me like that.

But, let's go down the hallway and sit together at the family room dining table. I will make us some tea. As you can see, the table has a knitting project on it. Let me explain: Mulan became determined to learn how to knit a couple of years ago. She badgered. *Let's take a class. It'll be so much fun.* I resisted. My resolve began to unravel. When Mulan became determined to knit, it seemed predetermined somehow. *Of course* I would have a daughter who wanted to knit. Maybe on some subconscious level she understands that the story of our trajectory toward each other has knitting in Act 1.

CHAPTER TWO

Just Tinking

I was thirty-seven and I was desperately in love with Joe. Joe is not his real name. In fact, let's call all the boys I fancied Joe, up until I met Michael. And let's give him a number, too—let's say he's . . . Joe #10.

Joe and I had been dating about two years. When we first met, I was diagnosed with cervical cancer and he had been an ardent and steadfast supporter through the whole ordeal. The cancer had left me without a uterus. But somehow, when the possibility of me actually carrying a child was gone, my desire to parent a child exploded. I'd nursed my brother Michael, who had his own cancer diagnosis (non-Hodgkins lymphoma), until he died. This tragedy had thrown me for an existential loop. I was devastated and unmoored after his death. A show business career suddenly seemed superficial and empty. After years of making decisions that led me away from being tied down in marriage and with children, I reversed course. Like most converts, my zeal was deep and unwavering. I wanted a husband and at least one child.

Problem: Convince Joe to get married and adopt a child with me.

Solution: Knit this man a sweater.

Okay, I wasn't the most skilled in the subtle art of obtaining a commitment. In fact, most of my time with men, up till then, had been spent perfecting the not-so-subtle skill of slinking away. I can only guess that at this moment in time, being thirty-seven, uterusless and insecure, but with energy (at least in my fingers), I deduced that a triumphant display of my abilities in the domestic arts would really close the deal. I would create clothing with *my own two hands!* His heart would warm toward me, literally, from the wool in the lovely sweater. How could he feel anything but overwhelming gratitude? Surely he would rush out and buy a ring.

My grandmother, Henrietta, taught me to knit in a very basic way when I was a kid. I never made anything useful, just practiced on scraps of yarn until I lost interest, which was probably pretty quickly. Henrietta knit in the American style, which means that you circle the yarn around the needle, like a man around his partner at a square dance.

When I learned to knit all over again, in Los Angeles, my

teacher, Suss, who is Swedish, taught me the European style. This method eliminates the big elaborate circle and instead you just grab the yarn from behind like you're kidnapping it while it's not looking. The European style is highly efficient and the American style is absurdly inefficient and even showy. It's as if, when Europeans first sailed to America, the boat ran into trouble and the only knitter who survived was eight years old and sadly, mentally handicapped, and it was she who taught the art of knitting to everyone in the New World and even the subsequent waves of knitters who arrived were too polite to point out her crazy style and then somehow, as these things are, the tradition was minted.

In any case, my Los Angeles knitting education took place in a little shop on Beverly Boulevard called Suss Design, owned by the aforementioned Suss. When I arrived at class I met about eight other women. We all sat around an enormous wood table while Suss directed us to start a project, "Something small. A hat. A thin scarf." But not for me: I wanted to start with a man's extra-large sweater.

Joe was from Pocatello, Idaho, and he worked for a company based in Seattle. His job was to install virtual reality games for archers in sporting good stores. This meant he was always on the move, but in between work installations he either stayed with me in L.A. or spent time back home in Pocatello, where his parents lived. Joe also had a son, Joe Jr., who was about six years old when we first got involved with each other. Joe Jr. lived with Joe's ex-wife in Logan, Utah, about an hour and a half from Pocatello.

Joe Jr. and I had a rocky start. His parents had split up when he was two years old, but he still didn't welcome a new woman in his father's life. Over time, however, we developed a mutual understanding. Joe Jr. had visited Los Angeles with Joe often. I'd visited with Joe Jr. in Pocatello several times, too. Since I'm from Spokane, Washington—a place relatively close to Pocatello, perhaps psychologically most of all—Joe's family and demeanor felt familiar and comfortable. Their lovely house felt like home.

So there I was knitting this man a sweater. Whenever I thought about sharing my desire for a baby with Joe, I kept my mouth shut and my fingers moving.

And it worked.

Joe smiled at me more frequently and we laughed more often. The sweater had quelled much of the angst inside me. I was a genius!

I knit. I knit and knit.

I knit all evening and then sometimes woke up in the night unable to sleep and kept on knitting. My agent joked that I could have been writing a salable screenplay but instead I was knitting a sweater. For my boyfriend. The one who didn't really want another kid. And who probably already had a sweater.

I knit while my classmates made their scarves and baby hats. I knit as they graduated to child-sized vests and funky hats. I knit and knit.

In the meantime, I got to know my fellow knitters. You can't eat while you knit; it's one of knitting's great attributes. Talking and knitting, however, is no problem. We poured out our souls. We knew each of each other's significant others. We knew each other's hopes and dreams. We knew each other's knitting mistakes and life mistakes. We celebrated each other's achievements: A scarf! A hat! Leg warmers! But I knitted away at this grand project of mine, this enlarging mass of navy blue, emerging from my own hands like a sea monster slowly pulling itself out of dark blue water.

For nearly a year I knit this sweater, and as I finished each section the class had a celebration. First, the front, then the back, then on to a sleeve. I'd hold the finished part above my head and kick up my legs and everyone would laugh. Each week, they would check in with me: "How's the left sleeve coming along?" We would toast with our glasses of white wine after each hurdle in the sweater.

When the day came that the sweater was finished for good, Suss opened a bottle of expensive champagne. We all toasted the sweater. Suss helped me sew a small leather patch on the inside: "To Joe. Love, Julia."

Then, like a newborn, the sweater was passed from woman to woman, all eight of them caressing it, inspecting it, putting it on, and dancing with my baby, the navy blue sweater.

So you see, even though I decided to knit the sweater for reasons that were, at best, unconscious, or at worst, passive-aggressive and possibly sinister, I was surprised by how much I enjoyed the process and the result. I couldn't wait to give Joe the sweater. I was thinking I might start a sweater for Joe Jr. next.

I finished when Joe was in Idaho on his autumn hunting trip. We'd planned for me to go up and stay with his parents, and that way I'd be there when he came out of the woods. To get there, we also had arranged that I would fly to Salt Lake City, rent a car, and drive to the town of Logan, where Joe Jr. lived. Joe Jr. wanted me to see his grade school. He was in fourth grade. By this time, Joe Jr. and I were getting very close.

After I got Joe Jr. from school, we went to his house so he

could pack his things for the weekend. I lay down on his bed while he packed. He began to go through his whole closet, item by item. He told me how each thing found its way into his possession: "I got this one at Christmas from my stepdad. I got this T-shirt when my cousin Josh outgrew it. My mom bought this sweater for me at Penney's." His small hand would display the item of clothing like Carol Merrill on *Let's Make a Deal.*

"This orange shirt is my favorite." "This blue shirt is my fourth favorite." I loved his eagerness, his awkwardness. This thorough cataloging of his clothes seemed to come from a combination of not knowing what else to say and a real desire to show me the innards of his world.

Then Joe Jr. and I drove to Joe's parents' house. Joe wasn't expected until the next day. I showed his mother the sweater I'd knit. She was a knitter, too, and she ran her fingers over the stitches approvingly.

Joe arrived home the next day and I gave him the sweater, which of course was not a surprise, since I'd been knitting non-stop for almost a year. He thanked me profusely, genuinely. He put the sweater on and admired its nice fit. He modeled it for his parents and Joe Jr. and we all laughed together and then ate some apple pie. The dream, people! The dream realized!

But then.

Late that night Joe and I began to quarrel. He wasn't going to be able to make it to L.A. the next week like he thought he would. In fact, he was unsure when he would be traveling back to L.A. The issue of a child came up in the wee hours of the morning, when both of us were so exhausted from arguing that we didn't know what day it was or what part of the day it was. "You don't need me," he said. "What do you need me for?"

"To be the father of our child," I replied.

I couldn't understand what he was talking about. He was already a father, and a good one. Why did he seem confused about what a father was needed for? He looked at me like I was an enemy. I felt like everything I said or did was received as a threat.

The next morning, we went out to breakfast at a Perkins Restaurant. If you don't know what one of these is, it's like a Denny's. The overhead lights are harshly fluorescent, and for some reason, this is an important detail. Maybe because I felt like I was being interrogated while simultaneously not being allowed to answer any questions. In other words, we sat in stunned, sad, tense, accusatory silence. I ordered oatmeal.

Then I got dumped. He said it was over between us. The end.

At first I felt I couldn't breathe and the whole world went topsy-turvy. I felt like I was on the movie poster of *Vertigo* and like Jimmy Stewart, I was falling backward. I pulled myself together and nodded, almost choking.

I had to drive the rental car back to Salt Lake City to fly back to L.A. On the drive I felt I'd been gutted. I was the animal he'd been trying to kill that week in the woods. In retrospect, I realized I'd been happily, obliviously careening toward an arrow with my name on it.

It was raining hard. I was crying hard. It seemed like the whole world was crying and my whole body was liquefying. In the official breakup conversation, the sweater wasn't mentioned, but I understood that knitting the sweater was a big mistake. I had made an embarrassing miscalculation. The sweater: a million yards of hopes and dreams—the yarn had been a noose around his neck, tightening with every knit and purl.

I got myself back to L.A. and managed to pull myself into the knitting class on Wednesday, arriving about ten minutes late. All eight women and Suss turned their happy faces toward me. "Well? What did he say about the sweater?" "He loved it," I told them. They all smiled and turned back to their own projects.

"And then he broke up with me," I added.

I can remember each micro-shift in their expressions, maybe five or six separate ones—they went from benign, good-hearted joy to confusion, to sadness, to open rage. "He what?" they said, nearly in unison, becoming a choir of furies. I felt the temperature in the room rise. The women's eyes widened, and their hair seemed animated, like the snaky locks of Medusa. I could feel the knitting needles in their hands ready for action, weapons of the first order. Ready to kill. They would drive their knitting needles through his heart; I just needed to say the word.

That was one of the most satisfying reactions I've ever gotten after delivering news, ever. Bless them and their sympathetic rage. I've frozen this image of these women, and it rests on top of the memory I've put away under Joe #10. They guard it, making sure I do not succumb to melancholy or self-reprimands over the debacle.

Soon after, I stopped knitting. I figured that was the end of that.

But alas, no. Here I am again.

Mulan and I recently took a "Mistakes" class together. We

learned how to "tink." *Tink* is *knit* spelled backward, and it means to undo mistakes. Mulan asked me, "Have you ever made a really huge knitting mistake?" I said I had. I told her the story of knitting the sweater for Joe. Her face wrinkled up in disapproval. "Why would you do that?" she asked. "It was obvious that he didn't want a sweater *or* a kid. Plus he already had a kid."

"I know!" I said. "That was a bad idea." I try to sound breezy, like: *life can be full of bad choices, but hey, you get over it.* I suspect she will not take as long as I did to understand the dynamics of romantic relationships. She is not a pleaser like I am. Even though that fact also drives me nuts. But all right, okay, I suspect it will spare her some heartache.

At home, Mulan and I knit as we watch TV at night. My husband, Michael, will sometimes cringe as he watches me knit—to him, the mindless repetition is unbearable and the opposite of relaxing. Maybe the specter of me in automaton mode, eyes dilated but distant, listening to the chatter of my own mind while my fingers move with machinelike precision, is frightening. Hell, writing that sentence was frightening.

Sometimes while I knit, my mind floats and I see scenes from my own knitting opera, the mistaken—miss taken—sweater for Joe. I will finish a row of purls and the image of Joe Jr. carefully describing the clothes in his closet will rise above the music. I'll see the sad drive from Pocatello to Salt Lake City. Joe's parents' basement TV room, its shag rug and paneled walls. The laughing, the apple pie.

About three or four years ago I did a show in Park City, Utah. After the performance a good-looking twenty-something guy waited to talk to me. It took me a moment to realize it was

Joe Jr. He'd grown into a handsome young man and was attending a nearby college. We reminisced and laughed and promised to email each other regularly.

I really liked him.

But I'm not going to knit him a sweater.

CHAPTER THREE

Channeling Food

I came home from Pocatello and assessed my situation. I was now nearly thirty-eight. I wanted to be a mother. I had no uterus, sure. But now I didn't even have a boyfriend. My heart was broken like never before. I felt physically weak. As blasphemous as this may sound, this breakup was harder than cancer. Part of me thought: Fine, just go there. If you are that sad, be friggin' sad. I had a few regular voice-over gigs that could sustain me financially with little need to leave the house. I let myself go down. I went way, way down. I understood how someone could die of a broken heart. My life seemed empty. I felt I had nothing. But then I realized, that was not true.

I had a sofa and a television.

I turned on the TV, and there was the Food Network flickering at me, beckoning me with its seductive power. Suddenly I had to have it on constantly—one show after another. Sarah Moulton answering callers' questions, Gale Gand making dessert, Alton Brown and his puns: they were all there to keep me company, to let me be around—but not eat—glorious food. I watched them all at an angle, because I was lying on my side. Sometimes when I had the energy to cry, tears from the top eye would river over my nose, along the ridge of my glasses, and then stream down the bottom lens, turning Bobby Flay into a Renoir painting.

I was in a dark wood. The right road lost.

I ruminated.

Particularly comforting was *Two Fat Ladies,* a British show featuring two elderly zaftig gals riding around on motorbikes and making things with butter and bacon. When one of the fat ladies, Jennifer, died, I watched the Food Network tribute for her, sobbing while eating an entire box of saltine crackers and drinking nearly a whole bottle of wine. I began to wonder if I was getting dehydrated from crying so much. I wondered if one should cry into a cup and then drink the tears back up again.

There should be a Food Network show just for people who've gone through excruciating breakups. The host would be a woman like Aunt Bea from *The Andy Griffith Show*. Every day she'd make slight variations of the same thing: mashed potatoes.

And she would say things like, "And what did he say to that?" And "Well, any man with half a brain would be crazy to let you get away! Well, I never!"

As I lay on the couch learning how to julienne carrots correctly, I contemplated my life and all the decisions I'd made and where I now stood. It dawned on me, that in the Irish, Catholic culture that I was raised in, my role was clearly meant to be that of the Barren Aunt.

My father had five Barren Aunts, his mother's sisters. They were all big round cat-eyeglass-wearing women from Chicago. When I moved here to Wilmette, I was surprised to find that most of these aunties were buried in a family tomb in Evanston, at the Calvary Catholic Cemetery, a place that I occasionally visit. Of course I don't know if any of these women were actually barren. But that was beside the point. They did not have children. They were career women and they showered their nieces and nephews with attention. I myself have three: Aunt Barbara, Aunt Shirley, and Aunt Bonnie.

The Barren Aunt is someone who, when they send you a book as a present, it's from a museum. And if they send you a sweater, it's a cashmere sweater wrapped by the department store. When the Barren Aunt asks you how you are, they look you in the eye and listen to every word. They inquire about school *meaningfully*. When you are a teenager, the Barren Aunt is someone you can ask, "That family that I'm from . . . they're crazy . . . right?" And the Barren Aunt says, "Yes. Yes, they are."

Fortunately I was already an aunt to two delightful kids, my brother Bill's children, Nick and Katie, who at that time were four and five years old, respectively. So, even though my relationship with Nick and Katie was already really important, it was suddenly even more important. In between Food Network shows, I started calling them more often. I went home to Spokane at Christmas and spent more time with them. We made a plan that during their school's next spring break, I would fly up to Spokane and hang out with them every day, all day. I thought, My need for my own child will *really* be out of my system after spending a whole week with two little kids.

Every day I was in Spokane, Nick, Katie, and I went swimming or Rollerblading or bicycling. When I had to leave at the end of the week, I found it excruciating. By the time I got home, I was missing them so much, I realized that for me, being the Barren Aunt was just not enough.

I got back on the sofa and turned on the Food Network. It was St. Patrick's Day, and Emeril was teaching me how to brine my own corned beef. It occurred to me that after watching this channel for so long, I'd never actually made anything. The Food Network had become cooking pornography to me.

So I decided to bake this green shamrock cake that my mom used to always make on St. Patrick's Day. You just use Duncan Hines white cake mix, cut the cake into the shape of a shamrock, and then put green icing on it and little green sprinkles that chip into the enamel of your teeth.

I always had such superior contempt for this cake when I was growing up—I mean, it's not even Irish. But my youthful superior contempt always balanced out my mother's unbridled enthusiasm for it. After admiring my creation, I thought, maybe I should invite some friends over to eat the cake. Then I thought, maybe I'm not ready for guests just yet. I mean, what if I suddenly had to be in the fetal position again, watching the Food Network? That could be very awkward for my guests.

So then, I just thought, I'll eat the cake.

Then I was all by myself, eating a cake.

And suddenly I was overwhelmed with such a deep explosion of need. It was like a gong clanged in my heart, and I realized that I just *had* to have a child of my own. Someone I could make a shamrock cake for, who would inherit my superior contempt, which would be balanced out by my new burgeoning zeal for it. And then maybe the child would have a child, too, who could carry on the family superior contempt.

It was true, if I had a child on my own, this kid would most likely never have a father, and that was sad because I had really lucked out in the father department myself. But I figured that if I could not provide a father for this child, or an example of a loving adult partnership, what I could provide was this: a home without a bad adult relationship in it. When I thought about it that way, it was a big plus. Even a gift.

Why couldn't I just adopt on my own? I realized I probably could. Did I really care that I shared DNA with my child? It was theoretically possible to harvest eggs from my still-intact ovaries and then hire someone to have the child for me.

What did I have, biologically, to pass on that was so important? My Irish heritage with its tendency toward alcoholism and depression? Skin so pale and pink that it might not fare well as the coming generations have to deal with increasing heat and searing sunlight?

On the other hand, if I did hire a surrogate to have my child, I would be able to send out an announcement to friends and relatives that could feature a picture of me and my arm around a pregnant woman, with this written across the top: SHE'S HAV-ING MY BABY! The idea of confusing all my acquaintances as to whether I was announcing I was coming out of the closet and/or having a child appealed to me. But no. No, no. I had to admit that I didn't care if I shared DNA with this child.

And frankly, I didn't want to add more people to the world. I think that the Hebrew god is regretting saying, "Go forth and multiply," when he looks down (albeit metaphorically) on our planet. I like to think he wishes he'd written, "Go forth and multiply *in a sustainable manner.*"

During the swirl of my coalescing decision, I got a call from my friend Bob, who asked if I wanted to meet him for dinner at a restaurant about two miles away. Bob wanted me to see Thai Elvis, this guy who does an impressive impersonation in a restaurant in Thai Town. Even though I hadn't been agreeing to meet with friends very often, and I had a belly full of my shamrock cake, I agreed.

When I got to the restaurant Bob had already ordered the papaya salad and fried morning glory and was discussing the curried frog legs with the waiter. I felt a surge of happiness. No, I didn't have a committed male partner to adopt a baby with. But I had wonderful friends, and if you added them all together they were more than the sum of their parts.

Bob and I dug in and I was suddenly aware that I was over the Food Network. I wanted real food. I was tired of just looking at it on TV. I told Bob about my plan to go ahead and adopt on my own. We toasted the new baby. He was genuinely thrilled. For the first time in many months, I felt calm and confident. I felt light as air, like a hundred-pound weight had been lifted off my shoulders.

I settled back into my seat, savoring the food and listening to "Hard Headed Woman." As I enjoyed the music, the company, and the food, it occurred to me that the green papaya salad and Thai Elvis proved unequivocally that you don't have to be ripe to be delicious, and you don't have to be the real deal to rock the house.

CHAPTER FOUR

China Sweeney

I tried to figure out what this whole single-woman-adopting thing was all about.

It quickly became clear that it was all about China.

China has a one-child-per-family policy. It's loosening up a bit now. The Chinese prefer sons because, traditionally, it's the boys who take care of the parents in their old age. This has meant that many Chinese girls have been abandoned. And, at the time I was adopting, China did not discriminate against single men or women who were seeking to adopt a baby. This made China ideal for me.

I immediately started the process with what they call a home study. It involves a lot of paperwork—getting three years of tax returns together and proving you have life insurance, for example. I had to get three friends to write letters about what a great parent I would be, and I had to have them notarized. I had to have a "home inspection"—which frankly got me a little frazzled. But my social worker assured me that if I had a roof over my head and a bar of soap in the bathroom, I would pass.

The inspector told me I had to get a five-foot fence around my pool. I had a small backyard in L.A.—and a really teensy pool off to one side. I asked, could it be four feet? He said no, children could hop over a four-foot fence. I argued that my daughter would be from China and would probably be really, really small. "Could I have an exception?" He didn't laugh. He frowned and wrote some things down in his notebook. I tried to rescue the awkwardness and said, "I guess what I really need to adopt right now is a desperately ingratiating tone!" Again, no laugh, just more scribbles in a notebook.

(Oh, for the record, when I told my gynecologist—a Lebanese doctor in Beverly Hills—that I was adopting from China, he said, "No! You should adopt from Brazil."

"Brazil?" I asked—temporarily thrown by his objection to my choice of country for adoption.

"Yes!" he said. "Brazilian babies laugh a lot. Asian babies are very serious. You're funny. You need a laughing baby."

"I'm not looking for an audience. I'm looking for a child to parent," I sputtered at him. Then I laughed. This was ridiculous. But my doctor didn't laugh. *He* was serious.)

I thought about names for the baby. This was a big deal for

me. The idea that I could control the actual vowels and conso-
nants that a person would forever be identified by was intoxicat-
ing. I tried to think of names that might have special meaning,
Michaela maybe—after my brother Michael who died, or Emma
after Jane Austen's Emma, or Claire after St. Claire (girlfriend of
St. Francis, and patron saint of television!). Maybe even Henrietta, after my beloved grandmother, called Hen for short. I could
make it Etta, after Etta James! My mind reeled.

My mother had begun calling me with her ideas for names.
And even though I have friends whose kids have these names,
and I love them, when my mother would suggest them, I *hated*
them. They all screamed, "I'm-From-China-Sweeney." Once I
picked up the phone, and without a "hello" my mother blurted
out, "How about Lily or Pearl?" One day she called bursting
with joy, "I've got it! China! Call her 'China'! China Sweeney."
I said, "Mom, I'm not going give her some cartoony-Chinese
name."

I got all my paperwork in and then cleared my work schedule
for several months during the fall of that year, when I figured I
would be traveling to China. But everything was taking longer
than expected. I decided to make use of the free time and spent
two and a half months traveling around China.

A month of that time, I was with my friend Bill, who works
for the Sierra Club and is an experienced backpacker. We planned
on backpacking as well as staying in cheap hotels. At one point
we were in Yunnan Province, which is in southwestern China.
There's a mountainous area just northwest of Lijang where three
great rivers nearly converge (the Yangtze, the Mekong, and the
Salween). It's a protected UNESCO World Heritage Site. We

were hiking in a fairly densely forested area and got lost. We wandered around for six or seven hours, only vaguely knowing where we might be, and hoping that the small village we were trying to visit would somehow appear.

Finally this boy, who was maybe fifteen years old, found us and tried to communicate. He was very curious. He spoke no English, but he gestured for us to follow him. We did. He took us to the house he shared with his parents. It consisted of one very small, dark room, with a gas grill in one corner and mats around the edges for beds.

The boy offered us a pear. As far as I could see there was only one pear. (I'm not saying there weren't other pears, and probably food was stored where I could not see it, but there was just one pear visible.) We accepted his offer. What is frozen in my memory is how he opened his pocketknife and peeled the pear—with such precision. It was delicate and deliberate. It was magical. The pear opened for us like a flower, and he offered us pieces.

I looked around the house taking it all in. My daughter might come from a home like this one. My daughter was not going to grow up in the land of her creation. The poignancy of the utter randomness of what was to come overtook me. I had to regulate my breathing so my tears would not arrive to embarrass me.

After we ate our pear, he took us to a very special place, Tiger Leaping Gorge, a scenic canyon on the Jinsha River, which is an upper tributary of the Yangtze. Even though this is a popular spot that we'd read about in guidebooks for hikers, there was no one else there. We sat together for a long time, whiling the rest of the day away. We learned the boy's name, or at least we thought we did. He pointed to himself and said what sounded like "Miur-shwa." We approximated it back, and after a few attempts he vigorously moved his head in an approving manner.

It came back to me with particular force: I was going to name someone. But what?

A week or so later, Bill and I were in Tibet, spending time touring through monasteries, and sometimes sleeping on monastery floors. There was always a Buddha on the altar, and the goddess Tara was by his side. I loved her story. Tara was brought into being when the Buddha cried for all the suffering in the world. His tear fell into a lotus flower and out sprang Tara, the goddess of compassion. Tara comes in many manifestations.

Bill flew back to the States and I went on to Bhutan for a couple of weeks of hiking. In every schoolhouse there were paintings of Tara, along with Jampelyang, the god of wisdom. I began to think about how Tara is also an Irish name. I mean, there are the Hills of Tara, and St. Tara, and even jewelry—Tara brooches. The idea of naming the baby Tara took hold. She would be Tara. Tara Sweeney. Of course! How could it be any other way? When I got back home to Los Angeles, I eagerly filled out my final adoption forms with the name I'd chosen.

In January, about a month before I was due to fly to China to pick up my daughter, I came home to several messages on my answering machine. It turned out that the Chinese government had a new policy regarding single people adopting children from their county: you had to prove you were not gay. My adoption facilitators had been leaving increasingly frantic messages about how this was the day that they assigned me a specific baby, but the assignment could not be finalized. I had to fax a notarized document, signed by someone who had known me for more than ten years, stating that I was not gay.

Ten years? What was that supposed to prove? My initial instinct was to reject the whole idea of providing such discriminatory and unimportant information. I wondered if the adoption would be called off if I did not comply. The phone messages seemed to imply that it would be.

I imagined calling old boyfriends and offering, begrudgingly, with an exaggerated comic gulp, to "prove" I wasn't gay in order for them to sign the document. Then I heard the final message from my facilitator: "Miss Sweeney, we waited all day to get a letter from you stating that you are no gay [yes, 'no gay'—that's how they phrased it] but then we convinced the officials that since you were married before [a brief starter marriage in my twenties with a divorce made in heaven], you're probably not gay. So they just went ahead and assigned a baby to you. Congratulations! You have been assigned a baby!"

I went from relieved, to euphoric, to concerned. What did they mean, they just "assigned me a baby"? I imagined a bunch of Chinese bureaucrats sitting around in the offices of the orphanage, bored and smoking, and feeling irritable. Finally, one of them barks, "Oh, hell, let's just assign her that cross-eyed drooly baby in the corner."

Not that I wouldn't be *thrilled* to have the cross-eyed drooly baby in the corner.

But is she the cross-eyed drooly baby in the corner?

CHAPTER FIVE

Strong and Beautiful

I didn't find out any details about the baby I was assigned until a couple of weeks before I was scheduled to leave for China. This is what I found out: She was seventeen months old. She was from a suburb of Guangzhou called Tian. I was given a form with a two-inch-square photograph of a baby with black hair standing straight up like she was Eraserhead. Her gaze was skeptical and somewhat menacing at the same time. Her expression, "Who the hell are *you*?"

I had asked two dear and long-loved friends to come with me: my friend Darcy, whom I've known since grade school, and who has two sons and a lot of baby experience, and my dear friend Jim, who is a film critic and lives in Seattle. I was going to be in great hands.

The baby was seventeen months old! This was a surprise. I'd been preparing myself for an infant, maybe six months old, but this child was a toddler. She might even be walking around already. I hadn't childproofed the inside of my house! I ran to the bookstore and bought *International Toddler Adoption* to read on the plane.

We were traveling with a group. Forty of us were going to Guangzhou to adopt nineteen babies. Most of us were in our thirties or forties, and childless. When we gathered for the first time at LAX, we all had these expressions on our faces, like, "This was such a good idea. In the abstract." And, maybe more accurately, "What the fuck are we doing?"

One couple had just found out that they were getting twins, which they hadn't requested or anticipated. The expectant mother, who already looked wiped at the prospect, joked, "I figure it must have been all those fertility drugs."

I laughed. It was true; almost every one of us had his or her own harrowing story of infertility. On the plane, I noticed that the twins' mother-in-waiting was reading *War and Peace*. I wondered how long it would be before any of us would be able to read a long, serious book like that again (although maybe Tolstoy is exactly the point of view needed for the long haul of parenting).

I opened *International Toddler Adoption*. I was promptly horrified. Each story involved a desperate attempt to put a positive spin on a terrible situation. "Mary Ann feels things are going much better now with little Rodney, even though Rodney's tried to burn the house down twice, and her husband has left her, and she had to quit her job. Some days, after she's held Rodney down during a thirty-minute tantrum, his eyes meet hers and she feels they've made a connection. Which makes it all worth it."

I began to hyperventilate. I was absolutely about to ruin my life. My heart raced. I could feel my heartbeat in my fingertips as they turned the pages of this book. I guess a lot can get screwed up in a kid in the first year or two of life. I blissfully, hopefully, and ignorantly thought I was going to be handed a blank slate. She'd have a predilection for spicy Cantonese food, sure, but she'd also surely blossom into a brilliant, fully realized person, molded by my kind and confident guidance.

Reading this book, I realized I'd been quite naïve. Things could be complicated. Perhaps nightmarish. What would I do? What if the rest of my life was a psychological arms race with an emotionally damaged child? Eventually I peeled my freaked-out mind off the underside of the overhead compartment and calmed myself down. I would survive.

The baby I was adopting was officially named Tian Mulan. Tian was the name of the town in which she was found, and was presumably from. This name was used as her "family name." Mulan was the name they'd given her at the orphanage. "Mu" means strong in Chinese, and "Lan" means beautiful. Even though I thought it was a lovely name, I couldn't let her keep it. I worked in Hollywood. *Mulan* was a popular Disney animated film. People would think it was the only Chinese name I could think of.

On the other hand, I didn't want to dismiss this name. Maybe someone in the orphanage really did think, when they first saw her, "strong" and "beautiful." I decided to make Mulan her middle name. Tara Mulan Sweeney. This is what I wrote on all the documents.

When we arrived at the hotel, our Chinese facilitators told us, "Come to ballroom tomorrow at ten, we give you babies." The next morning, all the nervous adults dutifully showed up in the hotel's garish gold ballroom. An officious Chinese gentleman standing next to me announced: "First we will begin to give you babies, then we also play *emotional music.*" He turned to me and said in a confidential yet offhand manner, "Last time we no play emotional music. Not as good." I wondered, "What's the emotional music? Maybe some ancient Chinese folk tune, orchestrated with lutes? Or a little Yo-Yo Ma?"

He placed a banged-up 1980s boom box on a table.

The facilitators herded everybody to one side of the room, and then they began the baby transaction process. Names were announced, and the adopting parent or parents were maneuvered to the other side of the room, facing the crowd. Then, from a door behind them through which they could not see, a Chinese facilitator appeared holding a baby above his head. The crowd saw the baby before the prospective parent(s) did. There was a game-show quality to the presentation, as each baby appeared from behind Door No. 1. It was hard not to imagine scenarios in which a particular baby's looks might cause the crowd to gasp or boo. But everyone was well-behaved, and of course the babies were beautiful.

Around the third or fourth baby handoff, the guy who was manning the boom box took his cue and pushed his button. Out of the speakers blared a tinny version of "My Heart Will Go On (Love Theme from *Titanic*)." And not even the Celine Dion version from the movie. This was a generic Chinese Muzak version scored for electronic instruments meant to sound like acoustic ones, or vice versa. It was hard to tell.

Sometimes when I find myself in an overpowering, emotionally charged situation I end up focusing on minutiae. During my first wedding we had a high mass in a large Catholic church full of guests. I spent the whole time absorbed by the threadbare red carpet on the altar. I can still see the weave now. Why they hadn't replaced it? When had this carpet been installed? Was the carpet installer Catholic? Did he install the carpet in the morning or afternoon?

I was about to be handed my child, and all I could think was, This is the *worst* emotional music. What an awful choice. When I get back to Los Angeles I'm going to send them some *really good* emotional music. This is not the right music for a scared, forty-one-year-old woman who knows nothing about babies and is about to be handed a toddler.

Before I knew it, my name was called. I went to the other side of the room.

They brought in a baby, and put her in my arms.

Baby. In my arms.

She looked up at me, quizzically. She was wearing a light yellow shirt featuring a bear happily piloting a helicopter. Written in black permanent ink on her left shoulder were some Chinese characters. She was also wearing thick red sweatpants, and written across the back were the same Chinese characters. Her square-shaped, pudgy feet were bare.

She tilted her head slightly as she took me in. I tilted my head slightly as I took her in. She felt dense, heavy even. Sturdy and build to last.

All the books say, "Don't expect to bond with your baby right away. This is just a person, like any other person. You'll bond over time as you get to know each other." To my surprise, I instantly felt a deep alliance.

She had a beautiful, distinctive little frown, gorgeous eyebrows, and full, pink, heart-shaped lips. Right away I could feel her vitality and health and her spirit—just the pure survivor in her. She immediately fell asleep in my arms, like, "Okay, all this pomp and ceremony is too much for me to deal with right now. I'm checking out." Or maybe she was lulled by the emotional music. Whatever it was, it caused a surge of affection in me. I've wanted to check out like that, too.

Darcy, Jim, and I took her to my hotel room, and then they left Tara and me alone to get to know each other. I handed her a little doll that my friend Wendy had given me. Tara grabbed it, stared into its face, and then up into mine. She was tentative, quiet, maybe even too quiet. There was a stillness in her that I hadn't noticed in other babies. She looked like she was either meditating or in shock.

Tara manipulated the doll in one hand for several minutes, moving it between her fingers. She would look back up at me from time to time. I tried hard not to have a maniacal grin on my face, which would—let's face it—be really frightening. I mimicked her own facial expressions: calm, looking around, glancing meaningfully and quizzically. She took a deep breath, like she might begin to cry, but didn't. Then she looked back down at the doll and brought her other hand up to it, moving it now with both hands.

I took in every inch of her. Her eyebrow hairs, the lashes on top and bottom of her eyes, her impossibly broad and chubby-red cheeks, her ears, her fingernails, her fingers, the back of her hands and how her fingers moved as she played with the little doll.

They'd put little cribs in the rooms, but that first night, I wanted to hold her and sleep with her. Then I figured she'd probably never slept with another person before, unless it was another infant. So I put her in the crib and tried to sleep. Both of us tossed and turned, but eventually I nodded off. I woke up in the middle of the night. I could see her there in the darkness, silently standing in her crib, staring at me with these piercing eyes. I whispered, "Here we go, baby."

She did not smile. She never smiled. We started calling her the girl who didn't smile. On the third day, I was videotaping her in our hotel room, just the two of us. That's when it happened. A shy grin. I wasn't sure if it was into the camera, or at me. Oh my God, I thought, this girl responds to cameras. It may be the best or worst of fates that she is about to fly to Hollywood, the city of cameras. I raised my head and looked directly into her eyes, furtively—not with dominance or too much interest. She smiled again. She smiled! I beamed back, giving her my big grin.

She immediately burst into tears. Oops, too scary.

But she let me hold her, and I felt her muscles relax.

I had conjured her and now, here she was.

CHAPTER SIX

Letters from Camp

I t's 103 degrees outside right now. This is not typical weather for midsummer Chicago. Unrelenting heat. The low is 80 degrees. I'm not sure what the humidity is, but it feels like 150 percent. We've had a week of this, and it isn't breaking. My friend Jim, the one who accompanied me to China to adopt Mulan, once said about New York City in August, "I feel like I'm walking around inside someone's mouth." I'd never heard a more perfect description. That's exactly what it feels like now.

I've been getting up at 5 A.M. and walking Arden to the beach—Lake Michigan—where we watch the sun rise (well, mostly we miss it by about ten minutes, but the sun is just above the horizon and looks like it's dragging the entire lake up into the thick heavy air) and then walk back again. (I shouldn't say "we" watch it, because Arden stares at me while I stare at the sky. He's not interested in sand and water; he wants bushes with squirrels and rabbits, so he'd like to get on with it, thank you very much.)

It takes an hour and twenty minutes to do this walk. When I arrive home, before 6:30 A.M., I'm drenched. Rivers of perspiration pour from the top of my head, and, as they find their way under my hat, create six or so tributaries that cascade, Niagara Falls–like, onto my shoulders. I have become my own ecosystem.

Then I do not leave the house for the rest of the day. No sitting outside at night. I am hunkered down inside, like it's winter and fifteen below zero. Michael will be coming home in two days and staying for three days before he takes off again. I will explain the appearance of husband/father Blum in due course, but for now, I would like to tell you that I have received my second letter (for this summer) from Mulan, who is, as I mentioned, at camp.

Mulan writes, "Dear Parents, I am really hungry so I should write this letter. I have made so many new friends. My counselors are nice. I need a pen. My favorite color is pink. My hair is in a ponytail. Love, Mulan."

Her first letter from camp, which arrived three days ago, read: "Dear Mom & Dad, I am having a lot of fun. I need a pen. It is my third day and I have done Arts and Crafts three times and this note is so I can eat. Mulan."

Mulan's camp requires her to prove she's written a letter home in order to get in line for dinner, so this explains how nearly all her letters start, which is to tell us how hungry she is and how this is the reason she is writing to us. The pink and ponytail information is well known by us, so this is filler advertising itself as news. She may have to show she's written a certain number of sentences.

And they say that letter writing is a lost art.

Oh, I should explain how Tara came to become Mulan, shouldn't I? Or how she was really never Tara to begin with. To do this, we must go back to those beginning months with Mulan, er . . . Tara. In fact, let's go back to the plane ride from China.

I had to be in China for two weeks, in order to complete all the legal documents for the adoption. The first week is basically about making the babies Chinese citizens, so that in the second week you can make them American citizens. We had to go to the U.S. Embassy to get visas and other documents for our new babies, which we were required to show upon arrival in the United States. We all went together on a large bus, forty-one adults and nineteen babies. There was a parking lot outside the embassy area that was just for people applying for visas to visit or move to the United States. And the parking lot was filled with people, hundreds, thousands—I couldn't tell exactly, but it looked like a football stadium's worth of people waiting in a very long, snaky line.

Our bus pulled up, and it felt like all those people instantly stopped talking and turned toward us, staring. We got out, the sound of our feet on the steps was loud and inelegant. I looked out at the queue; they were watching us. They were looking at the babies in our arms. My back stiffened at our naked display of privilege. We were kings and queens who'd pointed our fingers at random foundlings who we'd raise for our own amusement. For our own satisfaction. To quell our own beneficent inclination. Before the situation became intolerably uncomfortable (but in truth accentuating it) our facilitators indicated that we should move to the front of the line. We were whisked in, ahead of everyone else.

Finally, it was time for us to go home. Darcy had flown home earlier, but Jim was flying back to L.A. with me, and then on to Seattle. I put Tara in the empty seat next to me and fell into a deep sleep. Then, waking from a trancelike slumber, I felt a poking sensation on my shoulder. I returned to partial consciousness, not quite understanding where I was. Through groggy eyes, I detected a man hovering over my seat. He said, "Hey lady, your baby's on the floor."

What was he talking about?

I guessed he was probably referring to the baby I saw on the floor of the plane near my feet. The baby on the floor—oh fuck. My baby. I picked Tara up, and she began to cry. She'd been happily asleep down there. (For several weeks after I got home, I suffered post-traumatic half-nightmares, jerking awake in the night at the dream-sight of that man, bending over me and now malformed like the Hunchback of Notre Dame: "Hey lady, your baby is on the floor.")

At the airport, I was greeted by a new boyfriend, someone I'd begun seeing just before I left for China. But no. No, no. I don't want to get into that particular digression. I'm forcing the next Joe into chapter 10. Off he goes.

When Tara and I walked in the front door of my house—just the two of us—she walked in on her own. At seventeen months old, she was walking. This dramatic "threshold moment" was nothing like I thought it would be. I'd envisioned myself carrying an infant in a snuggly. I had truly acquired a person, and she entered her new home on her own two feet.

I introduced her to my two cats, gesturing, "Tara, this is Rita, and this is Val." Tara pointed at Rita and let out an earsplitting squeal of pure, unadulterated joy. Rita looked up at me with an expression that said: "Why would you do this to me? I've only been good to you." Then she made her way under the bed in the guest room and Tara took off after her. For the first few weeks I would watch Tara's little behind, stuck out from under the bed, legs flailing behind her as she tried desperately to grab for the cat. A couple of scratches later, Tara got the message, but she remained infatuated, the most undeterred of lovers.

We went to a lot of parks. I'd lived in Los Angeles for twenty years and had never noticed children's playgrounds. Suddenly with a toddler, they sprang out at me everywhere. People seem much more likely to approach you when you have a child, and that's both a great and frightening thing. Once someone asked me at the park, "Is her father Chinese?" And I said, "Yeah. I think so. I mean, it sure seems like it."

They would also go up to Tara and ask her for her name, and she just would stare at them blankly and say nothing. I would allow a short pause and then answer "Tara" for her. One day when she was almost three years old, an elderly man leaned over and asked, "What's your name, little girl?" I said, "Tara," and simultaneously I heard my daughter say in a clear, loud voice, "Mulan." She looked at me with a frown, as if to say, "You can call me Tara. But I answer to Mulan."

I had to give it up. She was Mulan.

After that, I replied "Mulan" when people asked her name. Their faces would freeze in a smile and they'd say, "You mean, like after the movie?" And I'd say in a gush, "No, no. That was her name in China. I wanted to name her—well, I did name her Tara, but . . . blah blah blah." I soon tired of that song and dance and eventually just answered emphatically and slowly, "Yes. After the movie."

Once, a man asked me, "Like after *Moulin Rouge?*"

I didn't get to name her in the end. All that frothy blather about the power of giving someone a name, about (read the following nasally, please) *dictating the sounds that will emanate from other people's mouths to identify my daughter,* was all for naught. A pretty good introductory lesson in parenting, I think.

Reading my journals from this time, I can see that I was very excited to "do" things with Mulan. We would wake up early, around six in the morning. We'd often go to Denny's for oatmeal, and then stop at the store. The grocery store was a great activity for us. Mulan would ride in the front of the cart, and I would hand her things to toss into the back. Then we'd go to the park, and I'd assist her on the climbing equipment and push her on the swing and help her go down the slide. We'd return home and empty the grocery bags (another good toddler activity: having her hand items from the paper bag to me, and she'd be absorbed watching me as I put them away). I'd make a snack and we'd get the extra-large Legos out and spread them across the living room floor. I'd glance at the clock after all this, and it would often read 10 A.M.

Ten A.M., people. Dear Lord. How is it that being with a child is so much fun and yet time passes so incredibly slowly?

I learned that being a mother takes a lot of energy.

Before I was a mother, whenever someone used to say something along the lines of how exhausting it was to be a parent of a young child, I would secretly think, Yeah—I won't be like that. I'm full of energy. I consider myself practically tireless. Motherhood's going to be a cakewalk for me.

They weren't talking about *that* kind of energy. They weren't referring to calorie-burning energy, although you do need plenty of that. It was more like the kind of emotional energy that is consumed by patience—the kind of energy you expend when you must continually concentrate on preventing yourself from exploding. Like when you patiently pick up the food that's been thrown on the floor, replace it, and then *that* food gets thrown on the floor. Every time. This is when you realize that it's probably better to give a baby just little bites of food, instead of a whole plate, because handing her a whole plate of food is like handing her a playground, and how could you have not realized that sooner and how come this wasn't in any of the books? That's the kind of energy we're talking about here.

Also during this time, I was very busy rewriting my entire childhood. Turns out, my childhood was probably not nearly as bad as I once thought it was. In fact, my newly revised attitude about my mother is that she did the best she could. It dawned on me that the main topic of a thousand hours of therapy had been wiped clean, just like that.

When Mulan was about twenty months old, she went through

a terrible time teething. She was up at night a lot, crying her eyes out. Neither one of us was getting any good sleep. One day I was talking to my friend Annabelle and we were comparing notes. She has a son who is about the same age as Mulan. He had been teething, too. As she is happily married, I said, "Wow, it must be nice to have someone there to help you in the night."

She said, "Yeah, yeah. It can go like that. It can also go like this: You wake up in the night because the baby is crying. You have your idea of how to handle it and your husband has his idea and they are mutually incompatible ideas. You start fighting about it. Now your baby is crying and you're in a big fight with your husband. Then you finally get up and go to your baby and comfort him and eventually he falls back to sleep. You tiptoe back into your bed, exhausted beyond all reckoning, and there's your husband. And he wants to fuck you."

"Oh God," I said. "That's much worse."

At the time, I was working, voicing the main character on an animated TV show. I spent many afternoons recording. One day I was talking to one of the writer-producers, who had three children all under the age of five. I said to him, with circles under my eyes and my head hanging low, "How do you do it? It's so hard. How, how do you do it?"

He whispered to me conspiratorially, "Get her on TV."

I was confused. I said, "What? Audition her for a television show?"

He said, "No, get her on TV. You know, *hooked* on the tube."

I was going to be one of those mothers who didn't allow any sugar or TV. I said, "Well, Mulan doesn't even look in the direction of the TV when I have it on at night. She thinks it's just a flickering light."

He said, "Keep it on. Direct her gaze. She'll pick it up."

He turned out to be right. I gained a whole new appreciation for TV.

In fact, TV turned out to be a godsend. Once she really liked TV, it was a fantastic carrot. Even right now, with Mulan at camp, my TiVo is piling up episodes of *iCarly* and *Cupcake Wars*. I encourage this. When we moved here to Wilmette, Michael came up with this great idea. Mulan could "earn" TV by reading or practicing piano. For every minute she did one of those activities, she got a minute of TV. Mulan was suddenly carrying a stopwatch with her at all times, and practicing piano constantly. She began to read and read. Now she is in a special piano program at Northwestern University that she had to audition for, and—at least to me, a not musically talented or trained person—seems quite accomplished. She plows through books and keeps a notebook adding up her time. She gets to reap the reward of TV on the weekends. Genius!

When I first discovered the rewards-and-punishments angle of parenting I didn't like it. This was not how I figured I would parent. I thought my child would acquiesce to my direction out of admiration and loyalty and love and mostly by seeing that to sacrifice short-term desires for longer terms goals was obviously best.

But, duh. That wasn't happening.

Eventually I felt like a Mom de Sade, trolling for ideas of how to create rewards and penalties. Once I was driving and Mulan was in the backseat, holding a doll close to her, smiling and say-ing, "Mommy, I love my doll, I love my doll so much." My first thought was, Oh you do, do you? Uh, huh. Good to know. Good. To. Know.

I was horrified. I said to my friend Chris, father of two chil-dren, "I'm a dreadful person. I've begun to think like a devious manipulator. I hate the carrot-and-stick parenting approach." Chris said to me, "No, no, don't think of it like that. It's not punishments and rewards. It's *incentives* and *disincentives*."

Instantly I felt much better, just from the word substitutions. I was merely creating situations where my child was incentivized and disincentivized! I was doing what any person would do in an intensely interactive relationship that was constantly evolving, hierarchical, loaded, often claustrophobic and highly emotional. One in which I was temporarily bigger and smarter.

Maybe smarter.

Well, now I've been home a week all by myself. I'm still bask-ing in the empty house, and that muscle has released somewhere deep inside. I've relaxed.

You'd think I might have begun to miss my family. But I don't. Really, I don't. I do walk into Mulan's room a couple of times a day, not because I yearn for her presence, but because it just seems proper. I have to make sure her room is still there, and didn't evaporate because no one's sleeping in the bed.

I forgot to mention that I'm still an active parent while every-one is gone. And my young charges are in the middle of quite a makeover. You see, our dining room has been set up as a mon-

arch butterfly nursery. Michael has grown milkweed in our backyard to attract them. When he's in town, he occasionally inspects
the leaves for eggs. He brings them into the house, still attached
to their leaf and stem. He puts these branches, with the eggs,
in a vase. Then he puts the whole thing inside a mesh butterfly
habitat that sits on the dining room table. The eggs hatch into
teeny caterpillars, and then they begin to eat. They munch and
munch. The leaves become skeletons; only their spines remain,
the chubby larva bending until they look like green-striped candy
canes. Because Michael is gone, it's my job to keep the caterpillars flush in fresh leaves. They chomp like there's no tomorrow.

Last night I figured I'd join them for dinner. I brought the
salad I picked up from Panera into the dining room and sat with
them. Just the eight of us, with our salads. I guess because of the
salads, I think they're all female. Sometimes the caterpillars take
a big bite of leaf and then, after chewing frantically, they take a
moment before they dig into the next bite as if to savor the taste,
or recover from the effort. I took a mindfulness eating class this
year, and I have to say, those larva appear to be postgraduates.
Impressive, I thought as I tried to savor my own leaves.

One of the seven caterpillars has already formed her chrysa-
lis, and she's hung from the ceiling of the mesh cage for a few
days now. Monarch chrysalises become translucent in their final
days, and I could see the orange and black stripes on her wings.

This morning I was greeted by a new butterfly, freshly
emerged from her pupa. When the butterflies emerge they fill
their wings with a fluid that causes them to stretch and enlarge.
The extra fluid from last night's birth has dripped onto the news-
print we have lining the floor of the cage. A *New York Times* arti-

cle describing a transportation bill that the U.S. Congress passed after a long political fight is now wet with monarch amniotic fluid. I imagine the butterfly thinking, Transportation bill! I'll show you transportation! She could fly all the way to Mexico. Tonight, after I write this, I'm going to take her out of her cage carefully, holding her wings together the way Michael showed me (cue Rachmaninoff's dramatic piano concerto #2 here) and I will let her go.

Her future is wide open. She could fly a very long way, or get eaten by a bird within the hour. The extreme humidity is going to reduce her chances. As for myself, I'll go into my comfy, cool, air-conditioned house.

But I won't think about her. Really, I won't.

WEEK TWO

❧

Independence

CHAPTER SEVEN

Three Chinese Nannies

I had to hire a nanny.

I was forty-two and had lived alone for most of twenty-one years, and even when I did live with someone, it wasn't a baby.

Well . . .

Okay, let's not go there now.

First, you should know that I'm a terrible boss. Maybe one reason is that I feel uncomfortable being in a position of authority. A more insightful observer might say I have a childish need for approval. I want people to like me, most of the time. I think this character defect makes it difficult to maintain authority over those I've hired to do work for me. The bottom line is this: I do not like to manage a staff.

Also, in a group, I find myself focusing on the one person who annoys me the most and then staring at this person in frozen disbelief. While I appear to be stupefied, I am actually conducting a rich inner monologue about their annoying personality. This is a counterproductive method for getting the most out of your employees.

I also tend to overthink everything to the point of existential paralysis. For example, I'll picture a task, and then I'll wonder—for a very long time—if I really couldn't just do this task myself, which leads to me wonder why I've hired someone and why I'm their boss at all, and why aren't they my boss? And what is the essential nature of the boss-employee relationship? What is the sine qua non of employeeness? Or of boss(y)ness? Eventually, I'll notice the clock and realize it's too late to address the task at all.

I also get confused about how much personal sharing is appropriate, especially if someone works in my home, where, by definition, everything is personal. I had a few personal assistants over the years and we always drifted into murky territory. When I would explain to them about a certain tricky personal relationship, one they would have to be aware of in order to handle it appropriately, I would then feel confused about how much I needed to know about their uncle Paul's emphysema. Is there a quid pro quo for listening?

My friend Kathy, who's had many long-term, happily

employed assistants over the years, once told me that when she hires someone she tells them: "Here are two tips for keeping your job: 1) Sharing. I may come in the door from time to time and tell a funny story. I will tell you a funny story about say, a salesperson, and you will listen. When I'm done, this does not mean that you can tell me your funny story about a salesperson. I'm your boss and that means *I'm the one who tells funny stories.* And 2) the more I know about your personal life, the sooner your job will come to an end. This is true even if I ask you about it, which I will, because I will become curious. Just keep that in mind."

Wow, that's advanced boss behavior. I don't think I could ever go that far.

The most important reason I'm reluctant to hire someone is that I have found that you have to be very organized to be a boss. This means that while an employee can relieve you of work, they also make work for you. For example, the employee will probably, eventually want to know what it is, exactly, that you hired them to do.

However, even in view of all this, I was initially optimistic about hiring a nanny. For one thing, the nature of the job was clear: take care of the kid. Second, it seemed common for people to hire child caretakers who didn't speak English as a first language, and maybe not even as a second language, and to me, this seemed ideal. I fantasized that my nanny and I would have very little interaction, seeing each other only when we punched in our time cards at shift change.

On the trip to China I met other single professional women who were also adopting and they had lined up nannies well in advance of traveling. I was in awe. I wondered how they knew the baby and the nanny would get along. While in China, I learned that there was a person in Los Angeles who specialized in placing Chinese nannies. I was told that this broker could even find nannies from the same province where your newly adopted baby had been born. I had toured Tian, the suburb of Guangzhou where my daughter had been found, and wondered if I should just bring a nanny home with me from China. In fact, it even occurred to me that Mulan's biological mother might need a job. I teetered on the edge of another moral-philosophical wormhole.

I wanted to have a Chinese nanny. I liked this idea because I wanted Mulan to learn to speak Chinese. In fact, she was probably already speaking Chinese. As she babbled in baby talk, I sometimes wondered if she was trying to tell me something important.

(A quick digression: At a Cantonese restaurant in San Francisco a few weeks after I adopted Mulan, a waitress told me that the sounds she was saying over and over again, sounds that I thought were cute Chinese versions of "ga-ga," sounds to which I responded mostly by smiling and tickling her, was actually a phrase. The phrase was "I am hungry. I am so very, very hungry." The waitress frowned at me and I strained through an "Oh, so that's it. Okay, well, I guess we should get some food over here, then." Followed by a nervous ho, ho, ho.)

My real plan was to just stay at home with Mulan until I got a job that necessitated a nanny, which would force me into hiring someone. I figured I could probably get away with not working for three or four months. However, soon after I got home from China, I was offered an acting job on a TV pilot that I couldn't turn down. Not only that, but it was going to be shot in Canada. I had to find someone quick, so I called the woman who specialized in Chinese nannies. She arranged a meeting with three different prospects over the course of one long evening.

The first applicant spoke perfect English and Mandarin. She was about thirty. She was a medical doctor who had left China and couldn't find work here. She answered phone calls in Mandarin twice during our interview, which I thought was bad form. I asked her if it was hard, as a trained medical doctor in China, and to be interviewing for nanny jobs here in the United States. She choked back tears. She told me then that she did not have a valid passport and was here illegally. This would be impossible, then, because I'd need her to fly out of the country with me. Her phone rang again, and she took it. A doctor is always on call.

The next interview was with a Chinese-American couple. The husband said they would be doing the nanny job jointly. The wife didn't speak at all. In fact, she wouldn't even make eye contact with me. The husband was very stern and without emotion of any kind. He told me that he disagreed with the American way of raising children, that children should be raised to "have respect" for their elders. He wanted to assure me that my daughter would be raised to do as she was told and not be like other American kids, "always chewing gum and watching TV." I waited for him to move on to the unsavory influences of Elvis and rock-and-roll music. I knew I couldn't hire them. Though occasionally when I notice Mulan watching her thirtieth rerun of the same episode of *The Suite Life of Zach & Cody* while chewing gum and jumping up and down on the sofa after she has been advised repeatedly not to do so, I wonder if I made a mistake not considering those two.

Lisa, the last applicant, was about fifty-five years old. She came from southern China, like Mulan. She spoke almost no English. But she spoke both Mandarin and Cantonese. Mulan began to cry during the interview. Lisa took her from me without any fanfare, and began to pat her back in this rhythmic way—firm yet comforting. Mulan immediately fell asleep in her arms. I offered her the job on the spot. She agreed. I said I'd pay her fifteen dollars an hour. She said she only needed ten an hour. I insisted on twenty dollars an hour. She said, okay, fifteen dollars an hour. That was it, I had my nanny.

I. Lisa.

Lisa barely spoke English. It was perfect. I knew nothing about her and her whole life was a mystery to me. I put five hundred dollars in a special wallet and gave it to Lisa for expenses for Mulan. She asked if I needed her to clean the house as well. I said, sure. Before I knew it, her husband was also accompanying her to work and he was scrubbing the kitchen floor. I asked Lisa what was happening. She said her husband loved to clean. I asked, "He *loves* to clean?" She said, "Yes, he loves to clean."

Lisa's husband's English made Lisa seem like a born-and-bred Los Angeleno. He literally did not speak one word of English. To make matters worse, he was not on speaking terms with Lisa.

Lisa asked me to write out a list of what I wanted done around the house and then she would translate it into Chinese. She asked me many questions about my list and then spent time translating it meticulously. This took a lot of time, sometimes an absurd amount. But I figured we were all on a steep learning curve that would eventually flatten out.

In my house in L.A., I have a little writing office in the backyard, detached from the house. One day I was in my office writing. I looked out the window and saw Lisa, her husband, and Mulan all dancing in a little circle singing a Chinese children's song.

I had adopted an entire Chinese family. First I got a baby. Then I got parents for the baby. This was simultaneously disturbing and fantastic.

One night I came home exhausted and collapsed on the couch next to Lisa. I'd been working twelve hours on something or other—I can't remember now what it was—but in any case, I was beat. Lisa sat next to me and took great pains to tell me that Mulan had learned a new song. I was pleased, but I yearned for more information. I was sad that I hadn't been there to witness it. I remember Lisa and I were sitting unusually close on the sofa. In my state of depletion, I had probably just plopped down too close, and Lisa was too polite to move over. There we were, smushed together, a perfectly odd couple. I thought, Is this what it has come down to? Is this the best intimate relationship for me, with an older Chinese woman who barely speaks English?

Lisa said quietly that she had something to tell me. She took out a piece of paper; which was filled with handwritten Chinese characters. She said she loved working for me but had decided to open a day-care center with her daughter at her home. In fact, her whole family was going to run the day-care center, with the exception of her husband, whom she was divorcing. She told me I could bring Mulan to her house if I needed to. She'd need to stop working for me in two months' time.

I thanked her and then felt overcome with sorrow. Lisa asked me if she could ask one more question. In a quiet, small voice, she asked, "How come you didn't have your own baby?" She looked deep into my eyes. She had this look of sad, confused concern, like, "You have good teeth. Why aren't you married?"

I said, "I can't. I had a problem. Cancer, and an operation. I can't have children."

"Oh . . . ," she said, shaking her head. "So that is why you are not married."

I half-snorted, thinking about Joe #10. When Lisa left, after two years of working for me, she handed me the little wallet in which I'd given her the five hundred dollars for expenses for Mulan. During this time we had traveled together to Vancouver three times and to New York City probably five or six times. The wallet contained $405.50.

Clearly Lisa was very good with money. I did end up driving Mulan out to her day-care center a few times, and Lisa continued to babysit for me when I was in a jam. Mulan, who was almost four years old by then, really loved her. Eventually she moved back to China, buying two houses in Kunming, the city that reminded me so much of San Francisco. She currently lives in one house and rents out the other. When I eventually take

Mulan back to China for a visit, we will definitely see Lisa. In fact, I cannot wait to see her again with Mulan.

II. The Manny

I had to hire another nanny. Mulan was now old enough to start attending preschool a few hours a day. I decided I wanted to change my nanny style. I was ready to hire someone part-time who would be more like a mother's helper than a full-on nanny.

But this meant hiring a new-mode nanny. I needed someone to be around me more—my sidekick and co-caretaker—and be there when I needed to slip out and write, or even just to go to the gym for an hour. With Lisa, it was really a handoff kind of situation. We didn't hang out with Mulan at the same time (unless you count me in my backyard office staring out at the window at the two of them while I was frozen in procrastination as "hanging out together").

Frankly, I really didn't want to spend time with someone I'd hired. I felt self-conscious being around Mulan with another caretaker—a *professional*—right there. On the other hand, if they weren't right there, easily accessible, there was no way to be with Mulan, and then to not be with Mulan, with the flexibility I required. I figured I could hire someone part-time, but I was still attached to the idea that Mulan could learn Chinese.

And that's how I wound up with the manny.

Toby was about thirty years old, half Irish and half Chinese. He had worked here and there as an assistant and he loved children. He was handsome. He was straight. And he spoke Mandarin.

During the interview, however, I found myself confused. Why did I find the idea of hiring this guy so weird? Did I have a bias, favoring women as the caretakers of babies? Did I have a bias that made me prefer that the men who took care of children be gay? Did I fear people would think I'd adopted a baby only to hire myself a handsome man to cart her around and be my companion? It seemed odd, but why was any of this stranger than having a female nanny running around with the baby and me?

My initial internal reaction to him was a flat-out no. But I hated myself for that, because I really couldn't think of a good reason not to hire this man. He had experience with children. He was smart and funny. I was not sexually attracted to him, in spite of his good looks—which was another good reason to hire him.

Plus, it was funny that he was Irish and Chinese. If Mulan and I found a way to produce our own mutual offspring, the result would have his combination of ethnicities. The only thing I could honestly say was that something in me didn't quite click with this guy. But I chalked it up to my preconceived notions.

I hired Toby for a two-week trial period—twenty hours a week. We continued to not really click. I rationalized that this was a good thing, a way of maintaining a proper employer-employee distance.

One day Mulan, Toby, and I went shopping at Whole Foods. We ran into an old boyfriend of mine (Joe #11, whom you'll meet later). Joe was wide-eyed and smiling, amazed to see Mulan a few years older. Toby was carrying Mulan behind me. As my old boyfriend and I conversed, I realized that he thought the manny was the new man in the Sweeney family. I was flustered at the prospect of explaining the relationships, and more embarrassed that this situation made me so uncomfortable. I stubbornly ignored the whole reality of the encounter—not introducing anybody in that obvious, awkward way so common among socially inept people like myself.

Either I was a stodgy old reactionary traditionalist, or I was pathetically desperate to seem open-minded and modern. I hated the notion that this whole thing would be so much easier for me if he were gay—or even if he were even just a little effeminate—or if he were much younger, or much, much older. I couldn't bring myself to hire him permanently. I couldn't have this life-size reminder of my own inadequacy following me around all the time. When the two weeks were up, I decided to move on . . .

. . . and into the worst nanny-decision I'd ever made.

III. The Chinese Pat

When she came to the door, I honestly thought she was a man. In my whole life I have never seen a woman look so much like a man. And this is saying something coming from me, someone who had assumed that role professionally on stage and screen.

I played this character on *Saturday Night Live* called "Pat." Pat is androgynous, but not in the typical David Bowie, Prince, or even k. d. lang kind of way. Pat is androgynous in an oblivious sort of way. One reason I invented the character of Pat was that I felt like I was encountering a type of androgyny that was not glamorous; it was the androgyny of the harried mother who has no time to take care of herself or the chip-eating male parking lot attendant who seems detached from the world of typical male and female appearances.

So you see, when I opened the door I was simultaneously the worst and best person to encounter this nanny applicant. The Chinese Pat had a low voice; she had very short hair, in a crew cut; she was chubby in a way that disguised the distinguishing sexual characteristics of her anatomy. However, the Chinese Pat was a woman. She was not transgendered. She told me about her life, which was extraordinary. She was born in southern China, and at age two she'd immigrated to Vietnam with her parents. When she was seven, after the American War, they emigrated again, this time to Paris. She could speak French, Mandarin, Cantonese, and Vietnamese. Not only that, she loved to cook. She said she was good at it.

I figured she was not really a nanny or a manny, so I called her the "anny." I immediately liked her. I thought it was so cool, her background. She told me about her girlfriend, a woman she'd been in a relationship with for four years, who worked at the Chinese Embassy downtown.

I hired her. I confess I loved that everyone thought she was a guy. I thought, Oh my God, I have found the absolute perfect nanny for me. The Chinese Pat had no idea I'd played a character on television whose whole look and demeanor was meant to convey gender confusion.

After a few months, I would allow the Chinese Pat's girlfriend to come over to the house as well, especially if I was going to be out late and most of their time was going to be spent sitting in my house while Mulan slept. I got a job offer in New York and I decided to take Mulan and the Chinese Pat along with me. When we went through security at the airport, she was tagged for additional screening. I realized that the female security worker thought she was male, and she signaled for another man to come over to do (excuse me, I cannot think of any other phrase) the pat-down.

I said something stupid and confusingly vague, like, "You don't have to do that! You don't have to do that!" The female security guard looked at me in an uncomprehending manner. I was too embarrassed to say anything else and watched helplessly as the male security officer began his body search and then realized that no, the original female security officer could do the job just fine.

I had started dating a guy who wanted us to go to Mexico City for a long weekend. (Joe #12, see chapter 10!) I liked this guy, but it wasn't love. In fact, it was the first time I dated someone without any desire to take the relationship further, or to stop it. I liked seeing him occasionally. I was finally having the type of relationship I'd always imagined Barbie having—not a casual fling, but somewhat steady. We weren't exclusive and neither of us wanted it to go any further. On the other hand, we both really liked to be with each other. Sometimes I wonder if I would have been able to have a relationship like that if I didn't have a kid. My theory is that having a child took all that loaded stuff off the table.

I'd never been to Mexico City. At first it seemed outrageous to go so far for a weekend, but he pointed out that Mexico City was a five-hour plane ride from L.A., just like New York City was. Going to New York for three days never seemed out of the question. So why not Mexico City? I hemmed and hawed and eventually decided to go. I had been working with the Chinese Pat for several months by then, and I felt comfortable leaving Mulan with her.

While in Mexico City, late on Saturday night, I got a phone call from my nanny. She was crying, and I could barely make out what she was saying other than "Mulan is okay. Mulan is okay." I have never before, or since, had such a feeling of alarm race through my body. The Chinese Pat said she'd been in a car accident with Mulan. The accident had been her fault; she'd driven through a red light. They were safely at my house, and the car had been towed. After reassurances that Mulan was okay, I hung up the phone. And burst into tears.

My boyfriend asked me what was wrong, and I couldn't tell him. I didn't want to tell him what was wrong. I wasn't even sure why—he would have been comforting and alarmed as well. He had come to care deeply for Mulan. My feeling was this: I am Mulan's mother, and you are not her father. You cannot share in this fear with me. This is my fear to bear all by myself. This is too big, too scary, too truly intimate to let you in.

I cried for what seemed like an eternity (but in reality was probably only a few minutes), unable to tell him what had happened. Then I did. And then I began calling to try to get on an earlier flight home.

Mulan really was fine. In fact, she didn't even remember the accident. Which seemed odd. She was four years old; she remembered things. I wondered if the Chinese Pat was actually alone in the car at the time of the accident. But then, where was Mulan?

74

With her girlfriend? Was she too afraid to tell me that? And how well did I really know the girlfriend?

My car was totaled, in that way in which a car doesn't look totally smashed but everyone agrees that it is not worth it to fix. My business manager took it upon himself to do a search on the driver's license of the Chinese Pat. You know, just to see if there'd been any previous accidents.

It tuned out she had two DUIs in the past three years and one misdemeanor for lewd conduct, which had occurred outside a bar.

Jeeszhus.

How could I have been so stupid, so careless? Just because I had a fondness for androgyny?

What really upset me were the DUIs, not the lewd conduct, which I couldn't be alarmed by until I had more information. Given that she was sexually ambiguous-looking, and given how conservative the police can be, that could have been from simply being at a gay bar, or even just trying to go into a woman's bathroom. There was no point in asking her about it; the DUIs trumped anything else. I didn't notice any obvious sign that she had a problem with alcohol. I didn't recall her ever even drinking around me. I didn't really know what her drinking story was. I didn't know if I could ask, since I was going to have to fire her anyway.

Because I come from a family with myriad drinking problems, I worried that I had overlooked indicators that another more perceptive person would have noticed. In the end I told her, "I discovered you have a history of drinking and driving citations—" She interrupted me and said, "I understand." It was awkward and terrible. I felt both angry at and sympathetic to her, two intertwined emotions with which I'd had a lot of experience growing up.

After the Chinese Pat debacle, I had another chance to shift my perspective about nannying and parenting. The truth was that I had changed. I had grown into parenting. It was easier and easier for me—or maybe not exactly easier; maybe I was more used to it. I settled into the job. And I had a deep realization, too. It occurred to me that if you adopt a child, and you aren't giving her your special cocktail of DNA, the only real thing you have to give her is your influence. All I could pass on to Mulan was my own, tactile, day-in, day-out mothering and caretaking.

Which meant that it made more sense for me to be with my daughter as much as possible, and less sense to work so much. I didn't want to be simply the supervisor, or the bystander, or the financier of my child's upbringing.

Fortunately, this deepening perspective coincided with something I hadn't expected. And it made a huge difference: Mulan became interesting.

Sure, she was interesting before. Sort of like how a stuffed animal is interesting.

No, that's not true. She was always much more interesting than that. But once she could talk, once she could understand what I was saying to her, and I could understand what she was saying to me—when we could have even slightly complex conversations, it was a whole new ball game.

Don't get me wrong, I love the chubby squishiness of infants and toddlers, the hilarity of their bumbling optimism, the smell of their skin and of course their abundant affection and need to be held. But after a while, it can get boring. Caring for infants is a lot like being a lifeguard—long periods of mind-numbing dullness, broken up by jolts of high adrenaline.

But Mulan was almost four, and we had begun to actually have an occasional, genuine laugh together. Not a peekaboo laugh, but a laugh based on an idea. It made me want to hang with her. Much more than, say, with an employee. I wouldn't claim I'm all that patient or perfectly maternal, but if Mulan and I were together all day we'd get into a nice groove.

There is a term I learned called "parallel play." It's how children often interact before they play "with" other kids. They just sort of play on their own, near other kids who are also playing on their own. It's supposed to be some sort of big accomplishment when a kid graduates from parallel play to interactive play.

Why is that? Parallel play seems to be such a wonderful thing. There are few things sweeter in this life than being in the same space with someone you love and each of you doing your own thing. Mulan and I learned to parallel play. I would lie on the floor and read *The New Yorker* and she would play with her Groovy Girls right next to me.

Here's the rub: we couldn't really do that if I were coming home from work all distracted with work in my head. That kind of parallel play intimacy only occurred when we'd been together for most of the day and we were in sync. I had a very hard time transitioning after coming home from a job. In fact, I don't really know how anyone does it.

The only thing to do was to basically stop work. Or more accurately, make caring for Mulan my work, and make earning money something I did on the side.

I began to doubt the idea of "quality" time. I was more into quantity time. I figured that if I spent much, much more time with Mulan, I wouldn't ever have to be a great mom in any given moment. It would average out. I hated the idea of having to catch up with her. I realized that if you don't get your kid out of school and ask her what's going on within ten minutes, the moment is gone; it's out of her head. Plus, my parenting style was more about hanging out and waiting for my child to bring up things she was thinking about, rather than me trying to squeeze some intimacy and communication out of her in a short amount of time.

Then, for my next parental epiphany, I realized my biggest advantage in getting Mulan to behave the way I wanted her to behave—at least after she was about four and could better comprehend that everyone else in the world was not just an extension of her—was if she actually *cared* what I thought. I know I went on a bit earlier about the benefits of carrots and sticks. And it's true that this did work. And I did and still am employing that particular strategy.

But there was something deeper going on. I realized that the secret ingredient to parenting was not effort or structure or even carrots and sticks. It was having a deep, intimate relationship with her based on truly being present. Not just physically, but emotionally. When she really cared what I thought we were able to get through ups and downs, to get through momentary parenting lapses and childhood tantrums and resistance.

The only way I could teach her how to have an intimate, deep relationship was to have one with her, and the only way to have one with her was to be with her a whole lot, and not in a forced, now-we-are-having-quality-time sort of way. But in a long, languorous, no-big-deal sort of way.

I could make changes in my life. I would only take writing jobs I could do at home, while Mulan was in preschool. I could reduce my expenses so I didn't need to work quite as much. But the reality was more mercurial. In show business, you work a lot and then you don't work at all. You swear off work and then get scared, so you want work and there isn't any and you get worried about money.

Eventually I realized I had to try again and hire someone. I still had a fantasy that Mulan would learn Chinese. But she turned out to be stubborn about it. When Lisa had spoken Mandarin to her, Mulan had understood every word but refused to answer in anything but English.

One day Mulan and I were driving (I swear, half my memories of parenting in Los Angeles are of driving). She was about four and a half by then. I said, "Well, Mu, we need to hire another nanny. I really want you to learn Chinese, and it seems like it makes it easier to be with someone who does speak Mandarin with you, so—"

"I'd rather learn Spanish," Mulan interrupted.

"Really?" I said. "Why?"

"To be honest, I think I'll use it more," she replied.

"That may be true," I admitted.

What really threw me was how Mulan was talking to me at that moment. She was a person, with opinions and preferences. I did end up hiring a few more nannies, including the most spectacular one, Frances. They were all English-speaking young girls in their early twenties who'd moved to Hollywood to find their destinies. And Mulan did learn some Spanish at school, and when we moved to Wilmette, she switched over to French. She's not fluent in any language other than English.

But oh boy, is she fluent in English.

CHAPTER EIGHT

Arden

This is how my dog came along and ruined Mulan's chances for a sibling.

You see, I started out as a cat person. There was a time when I was single and had four cats, which I guess officially made me a cat lady. I don't know why I wasn't more embarrassed about that back then.

Out of that group of four cats, only one is still around. Her name is Val and she's a small six-pounder. Now she's very old, seventeen or eighteen. She stays upstairs in our house here in Illinois. She sleeps most of the day and spends her evenings ranting about her life in deep guttural meows.

She's on my lap right now as I type, and my right arm is underneath her belly so I have to be careful as my fingers strike the keys. Mostly she likes to sit on the desk directly in front of my face and peer into the computer screen. This means I have to move my own head around to see what I'm typing. Sometimes she does a slow turn to me from the screen, like she has read what I've written. The look on her face is "You've gotta be kidding."

When comparing cats and dogs, one reason I prefer cats is that dogs are often overeager and subservient in a needy way, a way that makes me embarrassed for their dignity.

I like how cats are aloof. I like how they act like they don't give a shit if you're there or not.

When Mulan was about three years old, we went on a trip to Spokane to visit my parents. When we got back home to Los Angeles, I sat for a little while at the dining room table chatting with our neighbor, Marc, who'd been watching our house while we were away. The front door of the house was open.

A scrappy dog appeared in the doorway, the afternoon sun on his back. "Oh," Marc said. "Him. That dog started sleeping on your porch while you were gone."

The dog, as if waiting for his cue, walked over to me and sat at my feet. He was gross. He was mangy. He did not have a pleasing appearance. In fact, he was even a little scary-looking. He looked like the dogs in the *Mad Max* movies, vaguely dingoesque. He had jagged teeth and sometimes his upper lip would catch on the side of his mouth above his teeth, which made him appear to be sneering at me.

Ick.

"Why do you think he's sleeping on my porch?" I asked my neighbor.

"I don't know," he said. "I was thinking you might recognize him. He played with my dogs for one afternoon, but we don't want another dog."

I didn't want a dog, either. I hadn't always felt that way. The year before this, I had gone to an auction with a lot of big celebrities. I was cohosting the event. I drank a lot of wine and was having a good time. A darling little toy poodle came up for bid. No one bid on it. I said, "I'll start things off by bidding six hundred dollars myself!" No one else bid. At the end of the night, I brought him home.

I named him Pip. He proved to be unstable. He began to tear the house apart. He shredded Mulan's diapers—while she was still wearing them. He shredded everything else in sight. You know how they say audiences sometimes have a sense that certain shows or movies will turn out to be stinkers before they even open? Maybe powerful big celebrities have the same instincts about dogs (something that I, a lower-level celebrity who is mostly recognized for being the friend of someone's cousin, do not possess).

I hired an expert to help me cope with having a baby and a puppy at the same time. The expert said I should wear a water pistol everywhere, day and night, as if I were in a dog western. Whenever the dog did something I didn't like, I was to shoot water in his face. This dog was as small as a rat and moved just as quickly. I soon realized that I was not a good enough markswoman to hit the dog. My walls soon were stained with water and the dog seemed to be getting crazier and crazier.

Feeling my desperation, my father agreed to take the dog. I took Pip to Spokane and gave him to my dad, along with a beautiful cage and ten dog-training sessions with a reputable Spokane trainer. After three months my father called me and said, "I'm very sorry, Julia, but I have to send Pip back to you. I cannot connect with Pip, and I'm not sure why, I love dogs, but this dog . . . I can't manage to train him and yesterday I had an incident with him. . . ." My dad went on to tell me about the incident. You see, he was in declining health at this time, and he had an oxygen tank. Pip chewed through my dad's oxygen tubes, repeatedly. Once while he was on the phone, one of those old-fashioned phones with a cord, Pip got the oxygen tubes tangled in the phone cord and almost asphyxiated my father. He said he felt like he was in a Warner Bros. cartoon and the dog was out to get him.

My dad put Pip on a flight to Los Angeles. When I got him back, I made it my first priority to find him a new home. Fortunately, through a friend, I found a very wealthy couple who were willing to take the dog. They had a penthouse in Santa Monica with a wraparound terrace that looks out over the Pacific Ocean. The bottom line is that Pip lives better than you or I will ever live. Through my friend, I know that Pip is doted on. This was probably what Pip had in mind for himself all along.

So maybe you can understand how not-into-getting-a-dog I was when this ugly beast arrived on my doorstep. I felt absolutely nothing for this dog. Marc and I decided to give him a bath. The dog was terrified of water, and he cried and scratched both of us a lot. He didn't even look that much different after the bath.

We took his picture and put up some posters around the neighborhood. One person called to yell at us: "Don't you know that people take dogs to horrible dungeons where they are used in incredibly sadistic, painful experiments by evil scientists working for Procter and Gamble and they use posters like yours to find their victims?"

Wow. No, I wasn't aware of that. We promptly took down all our posters. No one else called us. It probably didn't help that in the picture the dog looked like he was about to eat a small child. We both agreed he looked like the Big Bad Wolf from "Little Red Riding Hood," only much shorter. The dog slept on the porch and eventually I let him in my backyard. I really should have known that was the beginning of the end.

Marc agreed to see if this dog could get along with his two dogs, both elderly boxers. Our stray played with his female boxer. He also peed all over Marc's house, on each piece of upholstered furniture—two or three times each—just to make sure his territory was indelibly marked. My neighbor's wife put her foot down and marked hers. They were not taking this dog.

We decided we had to name the dog something besides "the dog" or "this dog." I was reluctant, thinking that a name would individualize the dog, lend it the illusion of a more appealing personality, or cause Mulan to want us to keep him. So far, Mulan hated the dog. If Mulan was walking from the kitchen to the dining room with a plate of food in her hands, the dog would walk next to her, throwing his hip into her thigh. This had the effect of throwing her off balance so that some of the food would fall off the plate onto the floor. Smart. And annoying.

I did not let the dog sleep in the house; I only let him sleep in the backyard. One reason was that he did not get along well with my cat, Val. He wanted to eat her, and she did not want to be eaten. The doors to the house could no longer be open, and I had to be vigilant about keeping the dog and cat separated.

At night, this dog would figure out things to do. One night he pushed my garbage cans toward the fence, climbed on top of them, and then jumped over the fence so he could play with Marc's dogs. Smart, once again. But this is something I realized: You don't want a smart dog. You want a dumb dog. You want a *very* dumb dog, one that just lies there and can't figure much out. (I do not have this same attitude toward children. Yet, anyway.)

In the meantime I was getting ready for my second adoption.

Okay, now I have to tell you, I really thought it was criminal to have only one child. I still sort of feel this way now. In the very first interview with the social worker, I told her that I wanted to adopt a second child soon after the first one. I figured a kid needs another kid, so that when they're adults they can say to each other, "Our mom is crazy, right?" Or, "I can't handle Mom for Thanksgiving this year; you gotta take her." As a single mom it was even more important to me that my child have another person in the world to be in her family.

As soon as I got Mulan home from China I took the preliminary steps toward a second adoption. I wanted to adopt a boy and I knew there were two countries where it was easy for single Americans to adopt. One was Guatemala, and the other was Ethiopia.

Each night I read either about Guatemala or Ethiopia. When I learned that African boys were at the absolute bottom of the list of in-demand adoptees, I chose Ethiopia. I paid for another home study and gathered all the financial and personal information to restart the process. I was about halfway through, knowing a child would be assigned to me within six months or so. So, you see, I couldn't think about also adopting a dog at this time.

Dogs require an enormous amount of attention and work, and they can cost a lot, too. Many of the people I knew, especially childless couples, had dogs that were the focus of their lives. What made me so judgmental about those people was this fact: the dog is never going to vote. Dog owners are putting all this energy and money and investment into an animal that will come close to requiring the same amount of energy, money, and emotional investment that people put into their kids and, in the end, the dog is never going to be a contributing member of society (at least in a participatory democracy), never going to discover anything (that you'd want to brag about), never going to further mankind's quest for anything but squirrels, never do anything but flop around and drool all over themselves in admiration of the people who are housing them. Ten thousand years of symbiotic relationships between humans and canines and what do we have to show for it? Sit, stay, fetch, and poop bags on pocket-sized rolls. MORE KID, LESS DOG was my fantasy bumper sticker.

I began to ask around to see who might want to adopt this dog. People wanted to know what type of dog he was. I resisted the impulse to say, "An old, bitter, not housebroken, pee-marking dog with scary yellow teeth and a bad temper, that's what kind of dog." Jeez. I became elaborately enraged at those who wanted to know what type of dog it was. I felt the same way about dogs as I do about kids: what difference does it make? It was a dog, a canine. If it was a kid I'd found, people wouldn't want to know what race it was. Well, maybe they would, but they probably wouldn't have the nerve to ask, and I wouldn't have liked that, either.

In any case, I figured I should take the dog to a vet to find out what the hell he was.

The vet said the dog was a purebred.

"What?" I said.

"Yes, he looks like a blue heeler, which is an Australian cattle dog."

"Oh," I said, suddenly feeling more hostility toward this dog, now that he was a goddamn purebred. I got the dog his shots. The assistant came in and insisted that I give a name to the dog. I really didn't want to name the dog. Finally, I settled on naming him after the street we lived on: Arden. After all, it was already at the top of the form.

While doing sit-ups at my gym, I started a conversation with the guy doing sit-ups next to me. He said he knew a guy with a cattle ranch in central California who used cattle dogs like Arden. I was thrilled. You see, it had become apparent that Arden needed an enormous amount of exercise. I had taken him on a couple of walks, but if he didn't get the chance to go on at least an hour-long brisk walk every day, he became unmanageable. This seemed perfect. Cattle dogs are a working breed and that's exactly what Arden needed: a job.

"Your dog will think he died and went to hell if you bring

him to me," the cattle ranch guy barked into the phone. He described how he kept his dogs tied up all day, sometimes for three days at a time, and then they run the cows and he shoots little pellets at them to keep them herding the cattle. He said it would probably take at least two weeks to break Arden out of the cushy comfort zone he'd been lolling in at my Hollywood home.

"Oh, he's not that comfortable, I mean . . . he's a stray," I said. I glanced over at Arden, who was happily asleep on his back, sprawled over the expensive, big, cushy, overstuffed chair that Mulan and I used for reading books together. Arden rolled over a bit so his legs just hung out like he was at the end of a yoga class. A little drool made its way onto the arm cushion. "Uh, huh," I said. "Well, I guess I need to think about that."

Okay, so Arden needed exercise. I found a dog park, called Runyon Canyon, which is right in the middle of the city. There's a steep climb from the bottom of the canyon to the top, about a thousand feet in elevation. Once you're inside the park, it's all off-leash, which made the exercise much easier and more enjoyable for me. Plus there was a great reward of a view of the whole city when you got to the top. At first I would bring Mulan and carry her on my back in a backpack all the way up. When she turned four, she learned to hike the two and a half miles all by herself. We went daily. *Daily.*

That's when I figured I really had to quit my television-writing job.

Wow, this dog was expensive.

I still wasn't all that into this dog, but I figured it was providence that had thrown us together. The first time I realized I had feelings for him was when I returned home from a long day away and Arden was so happy to see me that he peed all over himself and pretty much everything else in the vicinity of the front door. By this time I had convinced—er, *trained*—him not to pee in the house and he knew it was wrong, which made my heart break when I saw him trying to lick up his own urine. He so wanted to be a good, dry dog.

I got accustomed to his face. I got used to his barking. I began to feel safer with him around.

Mulan and I planned a trip to Spokane to see family. Now added to the grueling ritual of getting out of town was the hassle of taking Arden to a kennel. When I look back on it, I don't know why I didn't just say to my whole family, we will not be traveling until Mulan is older. But I wasn't smart enough then to make things easier on myself. I'd pack up the car with Mulan and our suitcase, as well as the umbrella stroller and car seat, and Arden, along with his favorite things—his blanket, etc. We stopped at the kennel and dropped him off. Then I drove to airport short-term parking, where I put Mulan in the backpack I used to hike with her, and then put it on my back. Why? Because I couldn't push her in a stroller and pull the suitcase at the same time. We went in and checked the suitcase. Then we would head back to the car, drive out of short-term parking, and into long-term parking. Then I would put Mulan in the small umbrella stroller, leaving the backpack in the car. Why not just take the backpack and not the stroller, you might ask? Because in Spokane I would need a stroller, not only for my use but for my parents', too. I pushed the stroller, having strung the car seat across my back. (Strollers that doubled as car seats were too cumbersome for daily use and I never found any I liked.) I also carried my handbag/diaper bag. We got on the shuttle and off the shuttle. In and out of the umbrella stroller. The car seat straps flailing around. The kid often yelling. Can I just point out how many parts of this story require getting a toddler into and out of a strapped contraption? And this was all before we got to security. It was insane! At the time, however, I just felt proud I'd figured out how to do it on my own.

When we got inside the airport, I saw a single mother I knew who had two adopted Chinese children. Her younger daughter was the same age as Mulan. She was pushing a piled-high cart from the check-in desk to the security area. One kid was on top of the luggage, and the other one was under her arm. She was all alone. We had met at various events held by Chinese Children Adoption International and I knew she also had animals at home. I didn't say hello; I just observed her from a distance.

And the sight of her overwhelmed me. She looked so tired. She looked like Sisyphus pushing that cart. I froze. I was transported out of time. I almost felt I was looking at my future self.

I didn't know that I was saying something out loud. I just felt my lips moving. It was as if they were some other part of me. I looked down at my lips. Why were they doing that and what were they saying? A silent shrill, a squeak seemed to be emanating from my mouth. Then I recognized the words I was saying: "I cannot have two children. I cannot have two children. I cannot have two children on my own. And a dog."

I canceled the Ethiopian adoption. I think if I'd already been assigned a specific child, I wouldn't have called it off. But I felt I was still on the bubble, and I could still back out. It did feel wimpy. I'd spent my whole life up until then—really, I swear—

never even thinking, "I cannot . . ." or "that's too much." I saw myself as infinitely capable. I could always add to my life.

The dog had kicked my ass. The dog had thrown me against the wall. The dog was the straw, and the spine of my unlimited capacity for more was broken.

But here's the thing. Now I am firmly on the side of people with dogs. The great beauty of the dog is this: just when dogs get to be twelve or thirteen—generally, just when, if they were children, they would be scornfully demanding things from you (money, food, rides) while simultaneously telling you that you were full of shit, just at the cusp of the beginning of the agony, the dog dies. Okay, that in itself is not the beautiful thing, but I thought of it this way: Dogs have an evolutionarily refined ability to understand human gestures and vocal commands, but their brains never reach adolescence. They require a lot, but they don't make demands that are steeped in derision. They do not mock their loving elders. They have no concept of sarcasm or irony, yet they can still be smart and funny. They are, in fact, grateful for every scrap you toss their way, and every moment of attention you give them.

As the mother of a girl on the cusp of teendom, I now believe this dog is a beautiful thing.

CHAPTER NINE

Big Strollers Are Bad

Nonhuman primates are hairy all over and their babies can cling to them by grabbing on to their fur. At some point along the human evolution superhighway, we lost almost all our body hair. There's much debate about why we lost our hair, but I guess the leading theory is that our environment got very hot and dry and hair makes you warmer, and exposed skin can be cooled quickly with a minimum of perspiration. The other theory is that hairlessness reduced the infestations of bloodsucking lice, fleas, and ticks that promote disease. This theory posits that there was some kind of evolutionary bottleneck and the hairless people survived. I've heard scientists say that this may be one reason why the exposed hairless back is so sexually appealing to both sexes, in that it advertises the lack of lice.

The fact is, we became naked apes. For babies and mothers, it presented a problem. Babies liked to grab on to the hair of the mother or adult caretaker and hang on. What to do with this naked mama? One solution, for the mother, was to stand up and carry the damn kid. It could even have been the need to carry offspring with arms that accelerated bipedalism. (For reasons I cannot explain very well, that word, *bipedalism,* always sounds to me like an uncontrollable desire to have sex with bicycles.)

The bottom line is that, for at least a million years (which is how long it's been since humans lost their hair), human mothers carried their children. This could have encouraged birth spacing because it's difficult to carry more than one or two children at a time. It could have strengthened family ties because other adults could contribute by carrying a child. It probably even kept our ancestors fit, lean, and strong.

Another thing that's great about carrying your child is that you take up less space.

I was thinking about this as I was jockeying for a view of one of the jellyfish tanks at the Shedd Aquarium here in Chicago. The tanks have rather small windows that are maybe six feet across. There are several tanks and in each one they have a startlingly beautiful species of jellyfish. But I could not enjoy the exhibit as I wished to, because everywhere I looked there were strollers in my way. Big strollers: super-wide, almost Hummer-like in their obnoxiousness, a veritable trailer for their precious cargo. Some of the strollers were at least three feet wide, taking up half the available space for viewing the jellyfish. The mothers appeared both oblivious and entitled. Their children were often too young or too checked out to even register what it was they were supposed to be looking at. Many were fast asleep.

Worse, several of the mothers seemed exhausted and irritated, as if the problem was not their wide load of babydom but the rest of us people who were in the way. We were in the way of their precious baby's view of a starfish. We all dutifully stepped aside and made way for them. I probably wouldn't have felt pissy about doing this if junior had been over three months old and awake.

Big strollers are obnoxious. Big strollers make your fellow humans on the sidewalk, at the café, in an elevator dislike you intensely. Even if I still give you an *isn't your daughter such a darling* glance, I will feel dirty afterward.

There are small, narrow, umbrella strollers out there. They are remarkably efficient and narrow—did I mention their narrowness? They also collapse into the size of an umbrella—hence their name. They have straps so you can sling them over your shoulder and along your back, thereby taking up even less space.

My rage bubbled up recently in one of my favorite shops: Larchmont Beauty Center in Los Angeles. The aisles are narrow and the place is packed floor to ceiling with small objects shoved onto prongs—bobby pins, combs, barrettes, curlers, old-fashioned retro things, new hip cool things. It's what makes the place such a joy to be in; it's a curiosity shop for beauty. But as I contemplated whether to buy some hair gel, a mother with an extremely wide stroller turned down my aisle. A grinning baby with arms outstretched gleefully grabbed, with its peanut-butter-smeared fingers (or maybe it was pulverized Goldfish crackers), every object available at a height of two feet. I realized that I was going to have to move, and the mother looked at me with this horrendous self-involved, unaware smile, like, "What am I going to do? I'm a mother!" Her left hand was breezily holding her Starbucks cup, and written on the side of the cup, in black Sharpie, were so many instructions for its making; a percentage sign, various unintelligible letters and numbers. And above these was what I assumed was her name, written like a hurried dash across the top: Kitty. Of course her name was Kitty. She's not even Kat. She's Kitty.

And while we're on this subject, what about older kids in strollers? Children who are five, six, even seven years old—many of them are so relaxed and comfortable they have their legs crossed as they look out from their perch. Here comes the king! Here comes the queen!

It's truly perverse.

So I say to mothers and other caregivers: Pick up your damn kid. Carry them. Make them walk. Better yet, get them to carry stuff! It's a great workout and you can interact better with your kid. It will cut down on the shopping you do, you will accumulate less, fewer resources will be used up, and you will save money. It will make you physically fitter, so it will likely prolong your life. And think of it this way: if you live longer you will have more time to recoup on your investment on this annoying and energy-draining kid.

Thank you for letting me get this off my chest. My feelings about this have clearly taken up too much space in my brain. And so, now, I vow to let it go.

CHAPTER TEN

Three Boyfriends
and Reflections on a
High School Crush

We have come to the time where I am ready to discuss the romantic liaisons that I experienced when I was a new mother.

Among my notebooks, I came upon a fancier one—smaller, older, and covered with red plaid fabric. I hadn't looked inside in years. I opened the cover and was transported back to the early eighties, when I worked as an accountant at Columbia Pictures in Burbank, California. My first real job. The notebook contains several years' worth of New Year's resolutions. I cringe at the restrained but loopy Catholic-girl writing style. From year to year my list does not change very much. "Lose weight!" "Read more books, and less magazine articles!" "See more movies, watch less TV!"

"Do not get married and have children!!!"

That last one made me laugh because I was not in danger of getting married or having children, at least then. What's funny is that I felt so strongly about it that I felt I needed to write it down. *As a resolution.* I wasn't even dating anyone. I wasn't pursuing a particular career path at that time, either. Was I trying to convince myself to feel that way? Was I really wanting to get married and have children?

Then there's the issue of the overabundant exclamation points. Certainly one wouldn't have New Year's resolutions with anything but exclamation points, for what are New Year's resolutions anyway but a declaration of war, an emphatic stab of a flag into the sands of one's own personal desert of time that stretches out to the horizon.

When I was with Joe #10, I forgot that I ever had been a person who didn't want a traditional life with children and a husband. My journals remind me that I am a jumble of contradictions.

About three months before I was set to go to China to adopt Mulan, I met a man. Let's call him Joe #11. He was a successful fiction writer, really funny and very charming, and just sad enough to be interesting. He thought it was fantastic that I was adopting a baby.

I kept thinking, Isn't this just the way? Just when you move ahead with your life and stop waiting for some guy to be the key to it all, that's when it all comes together. Then I would nod to myself knowingly. Ha, ha.

When I got the date I was to travel to China, Joe #11 announced that he wanted to come with me. I was really, really tempted to let him come, as things were going so well between us. I felt cautiously optimistic about our long-term prospects. If he was *the* guy, and this baby would be ours to raise, why not let him be there from the start? On the other hand, if he wasn't the guy, letting him come would be impulsive and weird.

I was already feeling protective of my daughter, and I didn't want to imagine her as a teenager in her bedroom, perhaps looking at some old photos of the day she was adopted in China, and hearing her say, "There's me. There's my mom. Oh, and there's some guy my mom was dating at the time."

I didn't feel I could ask Joe #11 point-blank if we were going to be together for the long run. I couldn't ask because I didn't know how I felt about him! All I knew was that he was asking to come along, and he could get a ticket and he would be there. He seemed very enthusiastic. He was very, very cute. He really wanted to come to China. Oh dear. Oh dear.

In the end I said no. Looking back, I feel that the clarity of motherhood was already working wonders on my psyche. The old Julia would have been impetuous and gone for it. The new mother Julia was cautious.

We agreed that he would be there to pick us up from the airport when we got home. He would take us to my house, but then I wanted my daughter and I to come in through the door for the first time on our own. Therefore we planned for him to pick us up, drive us home, and drop us off but not come in. It seems odd to me, now, that we had this all planned out in advance. And yet, it was just the right thing.

Before I left on the trip, he came over to put the car seat in his car. I asked him, "Are you really going to drive around town with a car seat for two weeks?"

"Sure!" he said.

Wow. Great. Enticing. Confusing.

While I was in China, Joe #11 called often. I would tell him about the baby and I felt he was politely listening, waiting for his turn to tell me what was going on with him. He had come to rely on me to listen to him unload about his day. I was glad to do that, but I was also falling in love with someone else: my new baby. I wanted a boyfriend, and he was a good one. But I was also in the midst of a much bigger and unprecedented thing. I cut the phone contact down to a minimal amount.

When Mulan and I emerged from customs in L.A. to the waiting area, Joe #11 was there as promised, all smiles. When we got in the car, I put Mulan in the car seat and then, just reflexively, got in the backseat with her. Now I think this was an odd thing to do, but at the time I didn't even entertain the idea of not sitting right next to her. This little move spoke volumes, I think. It made Joe #11 "the driver," not "the boyfriend." I wanted to be sitting next to Mulan because it was her first experience in a car seat, and I was worried about how she was going to react.

Mulan began to cry. She was very unsettled by the newness of the situation. She took deeper breaths and cried harder and louder. One might call her crying "screeching." She screamed bloody murder for the entire forty-five-minute ride home. All I remember from that ride, besides trying desperately to calm her down, was my view from the backseat of Joe's clenched fists and white knuckles on the steering wheel. Not a good sign.

He brought us home, and as we agreed, he dropped us off and left. I didn't hear from him for a couple days. It was a little odd, but fine; I was in my own world, and it was just what I'd indicated that I wanted. I wasn't sure if he was giving me space because I wanted and needed it, or if he was trying to pull back. How are you supposed to act when you're dating someone who adopts a baby? There are no rulebooks for that sort of thing.

He hung out with the two of us a few times over the next several weeks. We once had a picnic together on the beach in Santa Monica. Another time we met at a restaurant and afterward walked along Third Street near La Cienega Boulevard and window-shopped, Mulan in a backpack. When I hired Lisa, and I was back from filming the pilot in Vancouver, he would ask me on proper dates. One night we met each other at a romantic Italian restaurant on Melrose, and I made sure I didn't dominate the conversation with baby talk. Afterward we were both waiting for our cars at the valet, and I said, "Hey, you should have breakfast with me and the baby sometime. It's really starting to get fun. We've been going to Denny's on Sunset Boulevard on Sunday mornings and we even have a favorite waitress."

He turned to me and said, "Julia, first of all, I have *had* breakfast with the two of you before. And second of all, I'm dating you, not your daughter." I'm embarrassed to report that my knee-jerk reaction in the moment was to apologize. I said, "Oh yes. Of course. Yes."

We stood there in strained silence, waiting for our cars. I looked at my watch and saw that I would get home in time to put Mulan to bed. I realized how excited I was to see her. I pulled myself together and stood up a little straighter. I said to Joe, "Actually, you *are* dating me and my daughter."

So, basically that was the end of Joe #11. I was sad.

But only for a few days.

Then about six months later I met Joe #12. We'd worked together on a radio show and then began to hang out. Joe was about seven years older than me, but in many ways he seemed much older. Not in looks—he was very handsome, and fit—but just in his style of life, I suppose. By then Lisa was a major part of my life.

Just in general, dating was weird. I mean that it was weirder than it had always been. Suddenly dating felt like it did when I went to school dances in high school. This is because there was so much organizing you had to do just to go on a date. People had to be notified (Lisa) and the times had to be established. You had to go when you said to others you would go and you had to come home at the time you told others when you would come home. Lisa was my de facto mother, as she smiled with my date in the living room while I threw on lipstick and combed my hair in the bathroom. I found myself hoping that Lisa thought he was a good guy like I hoped my parents would like a high school beau.

The best thing about Joe #12 was that I wasn't that into him. I liked him a lot, but we were never going to live together. He bothered me just enough that I felt safe. I wasn't going to fall in love. Fantastic. Best of all, we stopped going on dates and began to just hang around my house with Mulan.

Joe #12 was a surfer and musician who spent most of his time in the ocean. He'd grown up in Hawaii and when Mulan turned two years old we both went with him to Kauai and I met his life-long friends. He packed his things in a pillowcase. I kid you not. A pillowcase. When the plane to Hawaii had to sit on the runway for some mechanical checks for two hours before we were okayed to take off, Joe #12 took out his ukulele and sang Hawaiian cowboy songs (called *paniolo*) to the passengers. He stopped singing before people wanted him to and Mulan was thrilled to clap along with the music.

We stayed with his friends in Kauai who had surfboards and some of his clothes. I wouldn't call him a hippie, but I think a lot of people about ten years younger than I am would call him a hippie. (However, he was not a pothead. In fact all the potheads I know are definitely not hippies, they are suits—professionals who work in corporate jobs. I dunno, maybe it's a fluke of who I've met, but I'm just sayin'.)

Joe #12 was the kind of guy who, you'd find out from some random conversation with his friends, had spent a year in Guatemala, just, y'know, hanging out. Not really in one specific place. Then, in another random conversation I found out he had also spent six months in St. Petersburg, Russia, y'know, just hanging out. Just enjoying . . . St. Petersburg.

Wow. Wild.

Joe #12 was the guy I went to Mexico City with, when the Chinese Pat nanny totaled my car. While we were together, he gave up his apartment in Venice and bought an RV. His plan was to drive along the California coast, finding better and better places to surf and figuring out where to park his RV at night so he could be right there in the water when the sun came up. The last thing in the world he would have considered was having or being officially part of a family.

And yet.

He had an easy way with Mulan that I really loved. Sometimes we would spend whole days together and then take a nap, all three of us passed out on the bed. It really felt family-like. At the beach, he would be so careful with her in the water, and he liked to carry her on his shoulders and run along the waterline. One morning Mulan started saying, "Dada, dada," in his direction. I gave her a look like, "Ix-nay on the Addy-day, kid."

However, after about nine or ten months together, after one very luxurious three-person nap, I asked him casually, and yet pointedly, "Do you ever think you could be part of a family?" I realized that I had come to care deeply and even love this guy. But after I asked him this question, the air between us was suddenly dead. He said he needed some time to think about it.

A few days later, he came to me and said, "I love you. I really do love you. And I love your little girl, too. But I cannot . . . I cannot do that. I don't have a life that could be like that . . . No, I can't. I can't be *that* guy for you."

Even though everything was on a very easygoing basis between us, I felt that this conversation meant we had to shift. I guess I did want to be open to the right sort of person. Hanging out with him was enjoyable and fun, but it was stirring my feelings, feelings I did not want to have stirred up.

We decided to dial it all back. A lot.

Frankly, I was sad. I felt like I'd been through all this before, too many times. I got ready to be really, really sad. I got on the sofa and turned on the Food Network. I found that the shows on the Food Network had changed—from being about cooking to being about competitions with ringing bells and noticcably more men than women. They weren't the old cooking shows I remembered from my last breakup.

But something else surprised me deeply. Here I was in the sad position—on the sofa, with the TV on, in the fetal position, and I'd added a baby on the floor. But the surprise was this: I actually wasn't all that sad. Frankly, I was sad for Joe #12. I thought he was missing out.

I got up and turned off the TV.

I flew to Spokane with Mulan to go to my twenty-five-year high school reunion. As I walked into the auditorium I was surprised to see a boy I'd had a deep crush on in school. Actually I would say we had had a relationship, but I'm not sure he considered our make-out sessions and feverish debates about European history (we were in Advanced Placement European History together) a "relationship." In fact, looking back I have no idea what he was thinking, and I'll bet you money he certainly had no idea what he was thinking when it came to me.

So, I had this high school crush, and yes—let's call him Joe—I really fell for him. I thought he was brilliant and because he was brilliant I deduced he would be interested in a girl equally brilliant. I tried to cultivate an intentionally "smart" look. I purposefully failed an eye exam so I could get glasses. I think I was probably the only girl in the world who thought wearing glasses was really going to help make some guy fall for her. The reason I was in Advanced Placement European History in the first place was so I could sit next to him.

Occasionally, we'd talk on the phone for hours. Occasionally, we'd make out. But we were not boyfriend and girlfriend. I went to college at the University of Washington in Seattle and he stayed in Spokane and went to Gonzaga University and we wrote letters back and forth—I think I spent more time and effort writing him letters than I did writing term papers and essays for my classes. It wasn't that I didn't do well in my classes—I was doing fine. What I mean to say here is that the first time I really cared about every single word, about endlessly editing and waking up in the night vacillating about punctuation and paragraph structure, was when I was composing my letters to him.

I thought if you wrote a guy a letter that was witty, brilliant, thoughtful, and insightful about the whole world, well, he would surely fall in love with you. I remember writing him one letter that I was positive was going to win me a Pulitzer Prize, if only someone would submit it, which he would, after having read it, and also after proposing to me, because how could he let such a brilliant writer get away?

He worked part-time, late at night, at a Catholic funeral home in Spokane called Hennessey-Smith. I used to hang out with him there when I was in town. Hennessey-Smith's major competitor at the time was a place called Ball & Dodd, and their motto ("On Your Way to God, Stop at Ball & Dodd") generated much mirth among us Spokanites. Honestly, I wished Joe worked at Ball & Dodd, but how could I complain? I got to

see the backstage area of a funeral home. I would help him vac-
uum the casket rooms, and then we'd have passionate make-out
sessions.

I noticed that the room was divided between Irish-themed
caskets and Italian-themed ones. The Irish caskets were lined
with silk and printed with images of St. Patrick stepping on the
snake, a lovely tableau for the dead to gaze upon for the rest of
time. I didn't know if I'd want to look at a slithering snake while
underground, but then I wouldn't have wanted an Italian casket,
either, with its copy of Da Vinci's *Last Supper*. All that food and
no way to eat it, like watching a frozen version of the Food Network for all eternity.

Eventually we saw each other less and less. He ended up join-
ing the military. I went off and wondered for years, including
many hours with a therapist, why it was okay with me to be so
insignificant to someone. The bottom line was that to me he was
a very important person; he was truly my first love.

When I went to my ten-year high school reunion, Joe was
there, but he didn't behave or look at me any differently than he
did with anyone else in our class. By then I *mostly* didn't care.

At our twenty-year reunion he wasn't there and by then I
really didn't care.

By the twenty-fifth-year reunion, I had honestly not given
him a thought. So, you can imagine how surprised I was to find
Joe, making a beeline for me as soon as I entered the high school
gymnasium. His eyes were misty and filled with love. In fact,
the look on his face was more affectionate and passionate than
any look I'd ever witnessed on him before. He took my hand and
looked deeply in my face. He cleared his throat, emotionally.

He began, "My mother died a few months ago . . ." He stepped closer to me, within kissing distance, then continued: "And I went through the house and I found this box with all these letters you'd written me in college and . . . and . . . and. . . ."

"Yes?" I said.

"Wow, we were so close, you and I. Us. What a great pair."

I felt suspended in time. I wanted to transport myself back to age nineteen, and say, "See here, Julia. He did eventually care. The letters actually had the desired effect. Just twenty-five years too late!"

I looked into his face and said, "Yes." I smiled back at him but I felt stiff and awkward. I realized my smile had frozen and I gracelessly rearranged my expression to seem more natural. I felt a deep distance from this man, this blank person I had showered so much affection and attention on in college. Who are you? I thought.

Then I met his wife and I think I looked at pictures of his darling children, but I'm not sure; everything was a blank to me after hearing him say, "We were such a great pair." I think I looked like a deer blinking in the headlights.

A few months after this, I met another Joe. Let's call this one Joe #13. He lived in San Francisco. He worked for a nonprofit that focused on lefty politics, one that I greatly admired. He was handsome and smart and he got along well with Mulan. My friends liked him. I liked him, too. But I wasn't in love. I was about forty-three by then, and being infatuated with someone seemed like a brain state of the young and gullible. Not that I was cynical. I really wasn't. I just felt past all that. I thought that this was good, too. Cold, clear, honest eyes, that's what I felt I had. One weekend when I was in San Francisco he took me to a very romantic and expensive restaurant and proposed. I thought, Yes. This is good. I'm not in love with this guy, and that means I am making a good, logical choice in him of a mate. I'm so screwed up when it comes to falling for men that if I was falling for someone, that should indicate that I should run in the opposite direction! So this guy is perfect. He's nice, he's smart, I love his social and political views, I love his job, and he is so into me. I'm sure my love for him will grow over time.

I said, "Yes." We smiled deeply into each other's eyes. It was completely wonderful and everything I could have wished for. We were all dressed up. Looking at it from the outside, it was wildly romantic.

Then this thirst came upon me. It was so big and powerful. It felt like a wave and it had me right in its grip. The urge I had was to drink alcohol. I needed to drink some alcohol.

We ordered cocktails, and I asked that mine be a double. We toasted our union. I threw my drink back. I ordered another one. And then, as it turns out, many more. Everything got a bit hazy. I blacked out.

The next morning he told me that I'd vomited on him. *I'd vomited on him.* I was horrified; I'd never done anything like that before. He said he had to put me in the shower to clean me up. I felt so profoundly embarrassed and guilty that I doubled, no, I tripled (!) my commitment to him. I mean, after all, he'd seen me at my absolute worst. Blacking out? That was seriously crazy. I hadn't done that since I was in college. In fact, I can't remember doing something like that, ever. And yet, in spite of this humiliation, he still loved me. We would never speak of this night again, but I would devote the rest of my life to his happiness.

Soon after this I did a short run of a play in New York. My aunt Bonnie came and stayed with me, helping out babysitting Mulan at night when I did my shows. Bonnie spent her entire career as a counselor for low-income, troubled inner-city youth at a high school in Seattle. She's also been a therapist. She's the dream aunt for me because deep down, I too am a low-income, troubled inner-city youth.

I told her about my engagement. I told her I was so happy, but since Joe and I became engaged I felt an uncontrollable urge to drink hard liquor around him. She asked me if I thought anything was not exactly right between us. I told her I had only one complaint about him and that was that we didn't really have similar senses of humor. Worse, it was very important to him, not that I was funny, but that I thought *he* was funny. Because I had been known as a comedian, and worked with many comedians, it was a loaded issue. I felt constantly on the spot.

I will have you know that I don't need to be with a funny guy. Sure, I would like to be with a funny guy, but I don't *need* to be with a funny guy. Joe #12, for example, was not funny. I didn't care a bit. Joe #10 was not funny. And yet I was ready to walk to the ends of the earth for him.

What was hard was dating someone who wanted me to think he was funny, even though I frankly didn't . . . didn't . . . personally . . . exactly . . . find him all that funny. Everything else about our relationship was really good. This was just one teensy area. Was it a big deal? Was I petty to be thinking it was a big deal? "It wasn't a big deal, right?" I asked my aunt Bonnie. "I probably just need to have a heart-to-heart conversation about it with him, right?"

"You are a comedian," Bonnie said measuredly. "This is part of your profession. It's not *not* a big deal. I think it's a big deal. A *really* big deal."

Instantaneously, I knew she was right. I went back home and tried to talk to him about it. He got defensive, said he didn't know what I was talking about.

I won't rehash the whole Sturm und Drang. In the end, I had to break up with him. It was so horrible. I've done my share of breaking things off, but this one was the worst. I was the asshole.

I was confused about myself and about how I chose men. I figured something really was wrong with me. But I didn't know how wrong, and I didn't know how worried I should be about it. I didn't know how to be different, or in what way I should be different, and I wasn't sure I could change myself even if I wanted to change myself.

On top of all this, there was something else. It was this: I just didn't give a shit about guys anymore. They seemed to take a lot of energy and time.

So, I got out of the game.

That's the phrase I used when I talked to myself. It was as if a referee had blown a whistle and run at me with his black-and-white-striped uniform and pointed and yelled, "You're out!"

And my answer was, "Fine. That is perfectly fine with me."

Yes, I realized that Mulan would most likely not have a father. But so what? A lot of people don't have fathers. I figured I had a lot of really close and wonderful male friends, especially Gino and Jim, two men who were becoming an important part of Mulan's life.

I know you must think I'm setting this up to dramatize how I met my husband. And yes, I will tell you in a couple of chapters how I met him. And yes, I am in a delightfully romantic, and agreeable, working marriage.

But that isn't the surprise. There was a different big surprise. It was the best thing about "getting out of the game." It launched me into a deeply, and up to that point, most enjoyable two and a half years of my life.

I would say that since I was sixteen, I'd been either trying to get out of a romance or desperately trying to get someone to notice me. I had not spent any significant time as an adult not wanting any of it. And listen, people—it was great. I had no idea how much space men had taken up in my brain. I had no idea how much energy went into starting a romance, getting to know someone, and maintaining that relationship. I realized that I had all this emotional space back. I was surprised to find that I had so much energy all of a sudden, and so much more time. It was truly fantastic.

I wish I hadn't been so eager to be in a relationship. I wish my fears about being alone hadn't driven me to spend time with certain people. I wish I hadn't completely lost my self-worth with Joe #10.

I wish I could have had the attitude toward all those guys that I have about them now, which is an appreciation of the transitory nature of romantic relationships. I'm lucky to live in a time of unprecedented liberty and power for a woman. And I've taken advantage of that opportunity to make choices that many women—hell, many people—across the planet haven't been able to make. One of the results of this is that I got to know, intimately, a lot of really interesting and very different men. And when I use the word *intimately* I do not just mean sexually, although of course that is part of it, too. Now that I'm older, I wish I could take away all the anguish from my past relationships and have enjoyed them more, because they were very enjoyable.

Of course, that's easy to say now.

But I think that would have required a psychological perspective that would have been quite unlikely given my biology (in the end men really are sperm and women really are eggs), Catholic upbringing (in my mind, all my romances are scored with Bach's *Magnificat in D Major*, which does not allow for much lighthearted whimsy), my deep ambivalence ("Do not get married and have children!"), and desperation (let me knit you a sweater that takes up all my time while you decide if I'm right for you or not) mixed with independence (I can take care of myself).

CHAPTER ELEVEN

The Birds and the Bees

I remember asking my mother how babies were made. We were in the kitchen and my mom was preparing dinner. I think I'm about nine years old. My mother doesn't answer me but turns to my father and yells something. They both laugh. Then I have a memory of my father in a chair facing all four of us older children (I'm guessing ages six to nine) sitting thigh to thigh on the sofa in the living room. He says something about sperm in a man and eggs in a mother. I raise my hand and ask where the sperm is kept in the man. He says, "In . . . [long pause] his stomach."

Another memory: me talking to my mother soon after, and her asking me what my father said when I asked him this question. "The stomach!" she replied incredulously when I told her. "It's the [in a whisper] *penis*!"

I remember torn pages from a pornographic magazine passed around the playground at school, and pictures of men naked. So hairy. Ick. I remember a girl on the same playground telling us in graphic detail how sex happened. She added she knew about it firsthand because her brother and she had tried it. No one blinked an eye or thought that was weird, even though I also think no one got the idea that we should go home and do something like that with our brothers, or anyone else for that matter. We all agreed on the playground that the whole business seemed horrendous.

I do remember telling this sexually knowledgeable girl that there was another, less gross way to have a baby. The man and woman just slept in a bed together. The man's sperm could crawl over and go into the woman's vagina on its own. This was why there was that phrase "sleeping together." Otherwise, why would people say you had to get married before you "slept together"? I mean, duh.

I also have a memory of seeing a *Seventeen* magazine cover at a store and reading the title "Is Virginity Outdated?" And asking my mother while we drove together in the car what the word *virginity* meant. She told me that virginity was something that, if you didn't have it, no man would marry you.

That was it.

I wondered how I could get "virginity" because I definitely wanted to get married. But I didn't ask. The way my mother had said "no man would marry you" was emphatic and signaled the end of the discussion.

Then the time came where I, myself, was in a position of dispensing information about sex to a child who had no idea. Mulan was nine and in third grade. We were eating at one of our regular haunts, a fantastic Thai restaurant (not the one with the Thai Elvis) called Jitlada, on Sunset Boulevard. I am being specific for a reason. If you can, you must go and eat there. Seriously, stop reading this book, get yourself to Los Angeles. Don't miss the coconut mango salad or the soft-shelled crab in curry sauce.

But I digress. The point is that Mulan and I ate out a lot. My life seemed at that time to be a never-ending journey between her gymnastics classes and home. I think, when you're a single mother who primarily takes her nine-year-old daughter to dinner at restaurants, it's easy to think of yourselves as a couple. You eat, you talk, and sometimes you just stare at each other in a stupor of familiarity.

At Jitlada, we know the owner and chef, Jazz, who this night recommended the frog legs with green pepper and curry sauce. We politely declined. Perking up, Mulan told me that her class had begun studying frogs. In fact, she revealed she had a report to do and began to explain the basics of what she'd learned: "So, Mom. First, the frogs lay eggs, in a pond, and then the eggs turn into tadpoles and the tadpoles turn into more frogs."

I squinted my eyes. Biology—and science, in general— was not my academic strong suit. Only recently had I discovered my own deep, neglected interest in science, and had been scrambling to catch up with the twenty-first century. Whenever Mulan told me of anything she was learning in science, I'm sure I wore an expression of astonished bewilderment and surprise. My twelve years of Catholic schooling did not dwell long on biology (God didn't want us thinking about that) and avoided the subject of reproduction almost entirely.

Eventually I mumbled a response: "Uh . . . yeah. I think so. I think, though, that it's probably just the females that lay the eggs, and then the males fertilize them—although I don't know for sure—and there are probably all kinds of species of frogs with different ways of doing things. But yeah, in general, I'm willing to bet, the females are the ones with the eggs. Or something like that."

"Huh . . . ," Mulan said, listening carefully. "But, what does *fertilize* mean?"

I said, "Oh, the males have this substance inside them, and it's like a co-ingredient, called sperm. They sprinkle, or squirt it on the eggs. That's how they get fertilized. It takes both the female's eggs and the male's sperm, and together they make the new tadpoles." I was really proud of myself for the word *co-ingredient*. That was good.

"Soooooo, only the females have the eggs," Mulan said, her eyes wandering to the ceiling, taking this all in.

"Yes," I said.

"Humans, too?" she asked.

Let me freeze this scene for a moment and say that I considered myself an enlightened, open-minded, sex-is-no-big-deal parent, yet I hadn't truly prepared myself for this conversation. I had read a few parenting books and they all seemed to advise the same thing, which was, when your child starts to ask you about sex, or really anything that is complicated and multifaceted, just answer the exact question they ask. Nothing more. Don't elaborate. Don't overshare.

In that sense, I suppose I *was* prepared for this crucial rite of passage. I wasn't going to stop and take her hand, get all watery-eyed and explain the beautiful way that we create more children in the world. That wasn't what she was asking. She just wanted to know if human women had the eggs. The answer was clear and unambiguous.

"Yes," I said. I deliberately forced a pause. I tried to think of some other subject to move on to. I took a big bite of the mango salad we'd just been served.

Mulan asked, "Where do women keep their eggs?"

"Well," I said, "we women have evolved to have our own pond, right inside our own bodies. We lay our eggs in this pond, which is so convenient when you think about it compared to frogs, because we don't have to worry about any competing eggs. It's a pond of our own."

A pond of one's own. I imagined Virginia Woolf contentedly sitting in a pond of her own. And then drowning.

"Where is it?" Mulan asked, her eyes bigger than ever.

"It's in our lower abdomen, inside us, below our belly button, above our vagina." I had managed to be specific and totally vague all at once. Perfect.

"But . . . how do the eggs get fertilized?"

"By the man," I said, thinking why did I use the phrase "the man"? Aside from its conformist big-business connotations, I had possibly implied that there was only one man, some special Man who was used only for this purpose. Creepy and weird. And of course, incorrect.

Thankfully, at this moment the rest of our food was delivered. I scooped up some green beans with chili and hoped the subject would change. I realized my eyes were darting around, which reminded me of my own mother. I hated how awkward, embarrassed, and off-putting my mother became when faced with the subject of sex. Now my own body was displaying the same indications of unease. I took a deep breath and smiled in a *deliberately relaxed way* at Mulan.

"But how does the sperm get in to fertilize the eggs?" she asked. I said, "Oh, yes. That. Well, the sperm comes out of the man's penis and it goes into the woman's vagina. This happens when the two do what's called, 'have sex.' And that's where the egg—there's usually only one in the woman's pond at a time—gets fertilized." Only after the fact did I realize that I had said the words *penis* and *vagina* and *sex* in a strained, sotto voce tone. Just as my own mother would have done.

Self-hate swelled in my breast.

Mulan put down her fork. Her face was twisted in disgust. "That's where humans make a baby, where you go to the bathroom? Mom!" Her voice was rising.

"Yes," I said, looking around conspiratorially. "I know." I sighed. "It *is* weird. That part can take some getting used to."

"Gross," Mulan mumbled.

"Yeah, I know. As they say, it's like having a waste treatment plant right next to an amusement park. Terrible zoning."

"What?" Mulan said.

"The thing is," I went on, "that's how we evolved. That's where it all happens. And even though going to the bathroom and having sex are both in the same general area, they are actually totally separate." I wanted to add, "Except for some people for whom it gets all mushed together psychologically, which is sad and creepy in my opinion but certainly not morally wrong, and is actually understandable given the proximity." But that seemed to be getting ahead of the conversation, so I tried to change the direction slightly.

"Like your nose and your mouth," I ventured. "They're both close to each other on your face, but you wouldn't stick a bean sprout up your nose." Mulan gave me a pathetic lower-teeth-revealing smile and grunted a charity chuckle. Then she got back to the topic at hand.

"But Mom," Mulan began again with laser-beam focus, "how can this ever happen? I mean, men and women, they can never be naked together."

"Well," I explained, "when people are older—much, much older than a kid—when they are older and they both decide they want to, under certain circumstances, like if they're in love with each other, well, then, they can be naked together."

"But how do they know when?" Mulan asked. "Does the man say, 'Is now the time to take off my pants?' "

We held each other's gaze for a moment.

"Yes," I said. "That's exactly what they say."

To my great relief Mulan seemed content with that knowledge and began to eat with gusto. We moved on to other topics of conversation.

Later, as we drove home, Mulan seemed unusually quiet. I

glanced at her from time to time in my rearview mirror. She was sitting in the backseat, staring out the window. We were driving down Sunset Boulevard toward Vine Street and the sidewalks were filled with people.

Suddenly Mulan laughed.

"What?" I asked.

"Oh, Mom. You're going to laugh so hard."

"Why?"

"Because, Mom, you can't believe what I thought you said back at the restaurant. It's so funny. I thought you said that the man puts his penis in a woman's vagina—inside of it—and that's how people make a baby. Isn't that hysterical?"

A pause.

"That is what I said," I said.

"Oh," Mulan said. Her face had turned from gaiety to seriousness. There was a long quiet time. Mulan stared out the window taking all this in.

Mulan asked, "What if two people just walked up to each other on the street and started doing it?" Our eyes met in the mirror. Her eyebrows were furrowed and she broke our gaze and looked at some people standing outside Yogurtland.

At this point, I decided the best way to approach these questions was to pretend I was Margaret Mead, or some dispassionate anthropologist discussing the mating habits of a particular tribe. "The human species is very private when it comes to sex. Humans are unusual in this way. They have sex in private."

Mulan asked, "What if you went to a party and there were a bunch of men and women and they all just started doing it? Would that ever happen?"

"No," I lied. "That would never happen. Because humans are so private."

My back stiffened. I realized it stiffened like my grandmother, my mother's mother. I was reaching back, further back than my own mother's discomfort and into the graves of the next generation of discomfort. The dead live.

"Mom," Mulan said gravely, "have you ever done this?"

"Yes," I said, flatly.

"But Mom, you can't have children."

"That's true," I said.

"Well, you never have to do *that* again." Mulan sighed. She sounded relieved.

After a moment I said, "Well, if you really love someone and you're an adult, then you want to do it, even if you can't have a baby."

Silence. Mulan stared out the window deep in thought. "But Mom, how can people do that? I mean, how do their legs go? You know, not everyone can do the splits."

Ah, the perspective of the proud gymnast. Mulan became somewhat fixated on the role of legs in sex. She could not picture how it was physically possible, even if someone could do the splits. Finally, I said, "Mulan, people figure the legs out. They just do."

"Oh," Mulan said, taking this in. She quieted down and we got home. When we got out of the car, our cat Val was sitting in the front yard soaking up the last bits of sunlight. Val rolled onto her back.

"What about cats?" Mulan asked. "How do they do it?" "It's basically the same idea," I said. "But how do their legs go?"

Mulan wondered. "They, well, I think the male stands behind the female and . . . and . . . they just do, Mulan," I said, exasperated, and disappointed that "They just do" was the best I could do.

Once inside the house, Arden, delirious with glee at our return, jumped up and licked my hand. "What about *dogs*?" Mulan asked, having never considered the possibility before. "Same thing," I said. "It's basically the same thing for all mammals."

"But what about their legs?" Mulan asked again.

"Look," I said, now desperately tired of this subject, "I've lost my ability to describe it. Maybe we can look on Wikipedia or something and it will show us."

So we went to my office and got online. I googled "cats mating." And of course, on YouTube there were thousands of videos. We watched a couple of them. Mulan was riveted. She moved her face closer and closer to the monitor.

"Now what about dogs?" she asked. We watched a few dog videos. She put her hand on my arm.

I had another moment out of time. Like when you're in an accident, and time slows to a crawl. I could hear my own breathing as if I were suddenly wearing a space suit from *2001*. Mulan's hand seemed to be reaching out to my arm in slow motion: frame by frame. I believe I remember it this way because it wasn't until then, until this small, intimate gesture, this gesture of familiarity and of safety, that I realized where I'd led us.

"Mom, do you think there would be any videos of humans mating on the Internet?"

I am a monster. An incompetent monster of a mother.

I smiled and said firmly, "No. There would never be anything like that. Because humans are so private." And then, "Hey, how about some ice cream?"

Which of course was teaching her that when questions about sex get awkward, food is truly the answer.

Later that night Mulan asked, "What about Roger and Don; how do they do it?"

"I . . . , I don't know," I said.

All right, I was thrown. I thought I would have more time between frogs and same-sex intercourse than just an hour or two. I was out of my depth.

Mulan went to the bathroom and took a little longer than usual to come out. Later she said, casually, "I think I know how Roger and Don do it."

"Oh yeah?" I said.

"Yeah. Mom, there's another hole down there, where you also go to the bathroom. Maybe . . . you know, maybe they use that."

That's my girl, my Mulan, age nine, inventing anal sex. Smart, inquisitive, problem solving, Spock-like in objectivity and with a total lack of squeamishness. Bless her heart.

"Maybe," I answered her, and shrugged my shoulders to indicate: see how casual and easygoing I am?

"But Mom," she said, "what about two girls? What about Jill and Eve; how do they do it?"

"I . . . I . . . ," I answered meekly. I was beaten.

"Well, why don't you call Jill and ask her?" Mulan asked me.

"Nah," I said, pretending to be reading the newspaper.

Mulan put her face a few inches from mine. She looked disgusted with me. "Mom, aren't you even curious?"

CHAPTER TWELVE

A Fan Letter

About seven or eight years ago, I wrote a dramatic mono-
logue and I performed it for more than a year in New
York and Los Angeles. It was called *Letting Go of God*.
Ira Glass, who produces the public radio show *This American
Life*, asked me to record a segment for a show he was doing.
When this show aired, I got hundreds of emails from people.
They were flooding in, and it was hard to keep up with them.

At the time that my segment on *This American Life* aired, I
was working as a writer on the TV show *Desperate Housewives*. I
would run into my office between story meetings and read a new
flood of emails about my radio segment. It was thrilling.

The subject line from one of the emails caught my eye: "Desperately Seeking Sweeney-in-law." And the note said, "I am writing to you to propose marriage to you on behalf of my brother who doesn't know I'm writing to you. I would propose to you myself, but I'm gay and I live in San Francisco so I don't think it would work out between us. But I am proposing for my brother because his big deal-breaker with women is that they must *not* believe in God. They cannot be religious in any way. Everyone has their deal-breakers. That is his. When I saw your show, I knew you were the perfect woman for him."

The letter went on to inform me that his brother was a scientist who lived near Chicago. There was a picture and a phone number.

It was a funny, really well-written letter. And the picture featured a handsome man. I read it to the guys in the office next to me, but I didn't respond to it because—what was I going to say? All I wanted to say was "Hey. Great letter!" But I figured he'd say, "So, why don't you call my brother?" I wasn't going to call his brother who was a scientist in Chicago. C'mon.

Then I went to New York, where I was performing *Letting Go of God* off-Broadway. One day, after a show, I was turning in my microphone to the sound guy when I ran into a woman coming out of the restroom. She had just seen my show. She wasn't expecting to talk to me. She said, "Oh, my friend wrote you a letter several months ago, proposing marriage on behalf of his brother."

"Oh yeah, that's right," I said.

"I just want to vouch for those two," she said, "I've known them for thirty years, since high school, and they are really funny.

And smart. And Michael, the brother, he's cute and you should write him."

"Maybe I will," I said.

"You should," she said.

"Maybe I will!" I said.

"Do it!" she said.

But I didn't.

Then, several months later, I was doing the show again in Los Angeles. I came out after a performance and a tall, handsome man was waiting to talk to me in the lobby of the theater.

He said, "I'm Joel. I sent you a letter almost a year ago, proposing marriage on behalf of my brother."

"Oh yeah, that's right," I said. "I'm sorry I never wrote him."

There was an awkward pause. I thought about a sort-of crush I was developing with an acquaintance, which I knew was a bad idea. I liked my life free of romance. So I said, "Maybe I *will* write to him."

"Well, don't, because he's an asshole," he said.

I was shocked. "Oh dear. Why?" I asked.

"When he found out I wrote you that letter he got very angry with me. Even just today," he said, "when I was driving down here from San Francisco, I talked to Michael on my cell phone and I told him he shouldn't be mad at me because it was a good letter. And after you didn't respond, I even read the letter in a creative writing class I was taking. I accidentally left the letter on my chair and the next week a woman came up to me and said she found the letter and she asked if you had ever written to Michael. I said no and she said that was great because she wanted to introduce him to her daughter! But when I told Michael this he got even angrier with me than he had been before. He was livid that I was doing this to him and he yelled at me. So I just had to hang up on him."

"Oh my goodness!" I said.

"Not only that, everyone is mad at me for writing this letter. In fact, my mother is here visiting from Washington, D.C., and she just saw your show and now she's over there on the other side of the lobby. My mother really thinks this whole thing I did was crazy," he said.

"I have to meet your mother," I told him.

I went over and met the mother: Norma. She was standing with a friend of Joel's: Shyamala, who had also attended my performance. (In fact, it was really because of Shyamala that Joel was waiting for me in the lobby. After my show, all three of them had gone to Joel's car, but then Shyamala realized she needed to use the restroom. They waited for her as she came back in the theater to use the facilities. Then, as she was leaving the lobby again, she noticed I was there talking to people. When she got back to the car, she insisted that Joel come back in the theater and talk to me. Norma thought it was nuts, but accompanied them.)

That's how I found myself talking to all three of them.

Norma said to me, "You really shouldn't be talking to us. I told Joel that you were going to call the FBI on him for stalking you. It's so ridiculous that he wrote you that letter. I will say this, however: I would make a fabulous mother-in-law. I'm not the nosy type, and I don't get involved in my sons' lives at all. The most I would ever say to you is 'cute skirt' and by the way, where did you get that skirt?"

Oh my God, I loved her. Not that I was looking, but she did seem like good mother-in-law material to me.

I went home and found the email from the year before and I wrote to this Michael fellow and said, "Well, now I've met your brother, your mother, and your friend in New York. And I figured if you were half as charming as your brother I owe it to him, at least, to just say hello."

A few days later he wrote me back and the subject line was "I am mortified." He said he had never known the true meaning of *mortified* until he found out his brother had sent me that email and included his cell phone number in it, which caused him to get very upset. He had hoped that the email had been deleted by some efficient assistant of mine. He was terribly sorry that his brother had bothered me like that. His email ended with no encouragement of any further emails.

But I wrote back anyway. I said I thought it was fine, what his brother did. I told him his brother was really gracious and funny, and he shouldn't be angry with him. Michael responded.

I responded.

We responded.

We continued to respond.

After several weeks I gave him my phone number. He called immediately. His voice was like a whisper. It was simultaneously maddening and sexy. Marilyn Monroe meets Christopher Lloyd. But I got used to it. I wanted to know more about what he did. I could barely understand it. His work seemed complicated and mysterious, which was frankly a big turn-on.

But after a while, it seemed silly. I think I was just excited to talk to a scientist. What was seriously going to happen? A friend of mine warned against getting too wrapped up in emails. She said, "You never know about the chemistry between two people until you're in the same room. There's no way to know over the phone if this thing's got heat."

I wrote Michael an email, attempting to dial things down. I wrote, "I don't know about the emailing so much. Hey, next time you're in Los Angeles, let's go to lunch."

He wrote, "Well, I'm never in Los Angeles."

I wrote, "Okay. Well, see you when I see you, then."

He wrote, "I guess I *could* come to Los Angeles."

I wrote, "Sure, that'd be great. When?"

He wrote, "I don't know. How about tomorrow?"

Wow. This was very titillating and possibly frightening. I didn't know if he should know my address. What if he was weird? Did clocking in twenty-five hours on the phone mean you really knew someone? That night he called and I said, "Hmmm . . . I don't know if I should tell you where I live."

He said, "That's no problem. Tell me a restaurant and we can meet there."

I said, "But you could probably find out where I live easily on the Internet."

Michael clicked away on his computer, "Are you on Arden?"

"Yes," I said.

"I only looked that up just now," Michael said. "I don't think it should be so easy to find where people live. Complete strangers could find you." He seemed genuinely concerned for my welfare.

"Yes," I said, as I rolled my eyes. "That would be so wrong if just *anyone* could find me." I sighed, "All right, come and pick me up—I'll wait outside with my scary dog."

I got off the phone and began to google myself to find my address. It was the easiest piece of information to get. I began to google friends' addresses, including many famous people. Wow, their addresses were so easy to get! The only thing I could do to avoid Michael was to move, buy a place under a pseudonym, and then have all my mail go to a post office box. But I couldn't do that retroactively, and I couldn't do that in one day.

The next evening, Mulan and I sat together on the front steps as Michael drove up in a rented convertible. Mulan's eyes got big with excitement. At age six, she was already impressed by convertibles. Frighteningly so. He parked on the other side of the street. We watched him get out of the car. He was lanky and handsome. I liked how he moved.

We all walked to the Los Angeles Tennis Club together, the three of us. And of course, Arden. I belonged to the club, only a few blocks away. They had a Friday night kids program that Mulan liked to attend. Michael and I dropped her off and walked the dog for an hour through the neighborhood.

Michael owns a business that makes scientific instruments. My favorite story he told me that night was about fulfilling his biophysics PhD requirement to teach a class. Michael went to Harvard. His assignment, twice a week, was to teach a twenty-five-student section of a three-hundred-student lecture class. Michael found the whole idea of standing up in front of other people, talking, to be horrendous. Terrifying. He was filled with dread just thinking about it. He walked into his first classroom and faced his twenty-five students. Fear seized him. Taking one big, panicky breath, he began to talk, but then immediately turned his back to the students in order to write equations on the blackboard. He felt such relief, looking at the black slate, he didn't turn around again. For the entire one-hour-long class.

When he did turn around again, he discovered only three students remaining.

He only ever had those three students. One of those turned out to be one of the smartest students in the larger class. He got one of the highest marks on the midterm. Another one got the absolute lowest score in the entire larger class. The third was a divinity student who was so confused, and so ill-equipped to understand, and yet so earnest, he kept Michael after each session for thirty minutes.

After this traumatic experience, Michael knew that a career in academics was not his ideal career choice. Plus the grant writing that would be required for such a career made him even more uncomfortable than the teaching. What he really liked to do was build things. He always liked to work on cars, for example. He decided to develop his own version of a type of camera that could be used to understand the structure of proteins.

After our walk, I said, "There's a bar upstairs at the Tennis Club. Usually, while I wait for Mulan to be ready to go home, I sit in the bar and read my *New Scientist* magazine." I know that sounds flirty, and of course, I was flirting. But I really did do that on Fridays! I love that magazine. I still get it each week and I read it cover to cover, absorbing and understanding a good 10 to 12 percent.

Michael responded, "Well, I guess this week you'll just be bringing your new scientist." Good one. Cheeky.

Of course, when we actually got to the bar I had arranged for my friend Julia (yes, we are the two Julias) to *just happen* to be in the bar with her husband, Chris (of the "incentives and disincentives" discussion). We all sat together and had a drink. Chris is from upstate New York, and it turned out Michael's father was, too.

My friends approved.

More importantly, I approved.

We all approved of each other.

As we walked home with Mulan, she put her hand up to take Michael's as we crossed the street. Done. Done, done.

I was a goner.

He was a goner.

Mulan was a goner.

We were all goners.

We got married two years later, in a big blowout of a wedding. My family is Catholic and mostly disappointed that I am no longer one of the faithful. Michael's family is full of proud atheists from the Jewish tradition. In order to please our families, I got my friend Don Novello to officiate the wedding as Father Guido Sarducci, the character he played on *Saturday Night Live*. That seemed to satisfy everyone.

I can report with some confidence that a good time was had by all.

Sometimes I marvel at the fact that, if Shyamala hadn't had to use the bathroom that day after my show, none of this would have happened.

How we got to Wilmette is another story. In fact, part of Michael's dream (in fact possibly part of my allure!) was that I lived in Los Angeles, a place he lived in as a child for a couple of years. He'd always dreamed of residing in his beloved Los Angeles again. But no. We don't all get what we want. At least not all at the same time.

Writing that story was a good thing. I remembered. We've only been married for about five years now, and yet I already forget what a crazy miracle it was that we even met. When you have a kid, I think you're thrown into the kid business. Everything seems to be about mealtimes and when ballet starts and who's taking her to piano and when is the parent-teacher conference? We only have one kid, and I work at home, and it still seems chaotic to me, filled with appointments.

Michael is coming home tomorrow for three days. The only time we'll be together during this month. And likely the only time we'll be alone in the house together until next year. The time away from each other was good. I'm feeling gratitude. (I was going to write, "I feel grateful," but that sounds creepy somehow.) So let me say it this way: I appreciate him. I want him back. Bring him home.

And then send him away again.

CHAPTER THIRTEEN

Sphexy

Michael has been out of town, working. He came home from Tucson, Arizona three days ago, and he leaves tomorrow afternoon for Switzerland. I feel like a kid, and I think he does, too. When Mulan is at camp we joke that we are at *marriage camp*. Because we were parenting immediately upon meeting each other, we never had the normal time a couple has to just be alone together. When friends and family ask us how we're doing, I tell them we're running around naked day and night.

During one of these days, I came home from the grocery store only to find Michael missing. I figured he must have gone out. I sat down in a chair on the back porch and relaxed, reading for about fifteen minutes. My heart nearly hopped out of my chest when he stood up from the middle of some bushes, only a few feet away, holding an insect he had been quietly watching. It was a digger wasp, a bug of the genus Sphex.

Before I met Michael, the only scientists I knew were characters in movies. And the first movie we saw together as a couple was at the Los Angeles County Museum of Art. We saw *The Lady Eve* by Preston Sturges, and in it Henry Fonda plays Henry Pike, a scientist of the naïve and bumbling variety. "Scientists aren't like that," Michael said.

I nodded agreement, but inside I thought, Really?

Now that we live together I will point out to you that Michael has a butterfly net and a magnifying glass near the back door and his emergence from the bushes after a long quiet stillness is not atypical. I don't know why it still surprises me. But no, he's nothing like the Henry Pike character in *The Lady Eve*.

"This is the digger wasp!" Michael told me with enthusiasm. "You know—the insect that Daniel Dennett [philosopher and scientist at Tufts University] refers to when he argues against the existence of free will."

"Oh right," I said. "What was that about again?"

"This wasp makes a little nest to lay her eggs. To feed her offspring, she kills another insect by paralyzing it, dragging it into her nest, and then the digger wasp babies feed off the paralyzed insect slowly, until it dies."

"Oh God," I said. Suddenly an image popped in my head. It was of Mulan and me, just before she left for summer camp. We were in a Walgreens drugstore, late at night. I was so exhausted I could barely see straight. Mulan was full of energy and enthusiasm and as we walked down aisle after aisle she found things she needed to buy for camp. My slow, discombobulated slouch behind her forceful determination to pluck just the right items off the shelves made me imagine that we had a tube connecting us. In this tube, all my chi—my life force—was flowing steadily into her. The more energetic she appeared, the increasingly tired I felt. I was the insect being fed upon.

"No," Michael said, patiently, "not like that. It's because of this programmed behavior that digger wasps have when they kill their prey."

"Oh," I said.

"You see," Michael went on, "the digger wasps have this ritual they perform where they leave their paralyzed prey outside the nest and go inside and inspect it before coming back out and dragging the victim in. But if an experimenter moves the prey, the digger wasp will quickly find it and bring it back, but here's the thing: it begins its ritual again!"

"Uh, huh," I said, marveling at his enthusiasm "Which is what again?"

"The wasp goes into the nest and inspects it again, like the first time never happened," Michael said. "In fact, an experimenter can do this unlimited times, and the wasp will do the same thing every time."

"Oh . . . ," I said slowly, putting it all together.

"I guess the idea is that seemingly premeditated behavior is really just mindless repetition that has evolved in the brain of the wasp," Michael helpfully explained.

"The opposite of free will," I said.

"Yes. The opposite of free will," he said.

I turned and went into the kitchen. I automatically began to unload the dishwasher, but then, because I was thinking about the concept of free will, I decided to stop. Then I decided to have a glass of wine, which is what I always do when I realize I'm automatically emptying the dishwasher.

WEEK THREE

❧

Death

CHAPTER FOURTEEN

The Decline and Fall of Practically Everybody

Okay, let me stop this lightly comic, chatty memoir and bring things to a dead stop. Emphasis on dead.

My brother Bill died yesterday. It was not unexpected as he's had chronic problems with drugs and alcohol. But somehow, this feels like a complete surprise. I feel spent and tired; my grief makes me want to quit all writing and also write my way into some clear blue light.

I'm home all alone and I am so glad and very unhappy about that. Michael is in Europe. Mulan is still at camp, of course. I am just here with this enormous ball of weight pushing into my chest. It's suffocating and heavy. Michael said to me on the phone when I told him, "It's probably even more disturbing for you than you are capable of realizing right now. I mean, that probably would be true for anyone."

Yes, I agree.

I want to write about Bill, but first, I need to lie down.

Bill had been in and out of rehab for most of his adult life. He had also had many accidents related to his lifestyle and habits. Just this spring, he spent sixty days in the hospital with MRSA, a staph infection that is resistant to most antibiotics. He acquired MRSA from a stay in the hospital years ago, which I understand is now a common problem. Over many years, my brother Bill had been in so much emotional and physical trouble, I came to think of him as impervious. Immortal even. I think that if I treated my body like Bill did almost every day of his adult life, I would die after only one day. After many years, judgment and resentment slowly gave way to other feelings toward Bill. His tragic resilience was impressive. Expecting Bill to die had been a way of life for me. It allowed me to imagine that it would never actually happen.

My brother Bill and I were downtown, in Spokane, just a month ago. Bill appeared sober to me, but very weak. We'd run an errand and felt hungry for lunch. I told him I'd get something for us to eat. I looked across the street and saw a place called the Pita Pit. I said he could wait for me in the car.

Inside, I discovered that the line was long. I called Bill's cell and asked what he wanted, reading a list of menu items. "Well, the chicken souvlaki, of course," he replied. We both laughed simultaneously at the memory.

So, even though this story I'm going to tell you features, as its main event, my brother Bill throwing up, and this might seem inappropriate now that he has just died, I will recount it because for Bill and me this was a happy memory of a very difficult moment in a wonderful sea of adventure.

You see, in the summer of 1981 Bill and I went backpacking all around Europe. It was our first experience abroad. We each had about eleven hundred dollars that we expected to last us three months, or maybe more. After two months we ended up in Greece, where we spent nearly a month on the island of Santorini, almost totally broke. We found a family that would house us for a week if we helped them with their grape harvest. We worked picking grapes and even helped them stomp on the grapes—barefoot—on top of a big ancient-seeming pit, with long, intertwined twigs underneath us. The grape juice flowed into a big vat below.

One night, one of the patriarchs of this family, who had only one arm, deftly made us scrambled eggs with feta cheese for dinner. The family's grandmother poured ouzo from a big white jug. Bill was smiling from ear to ear. We were *really* far from home.

Back in Athens for a few days, we decided to take a bus to London (through Serbia, Bosnia, Austria, and Germany, and then the bus loaded onto a boat to England) that cost fifty dollars a person. The bus would take more than thirty-two hours of nonstop driving. It was also packed. There were so many people

145

crowding to get on that some people made bargains with others to alternate standing and sitting.

As we were waiting in line for the bus, I looked in my backpack and saw a wrapped package of chicken souvlaki I'd bought on the street the day before, or maybe it was even two days before. I was going to toss it out, but Bill said, "Hey, I'll eat it." And he did. (Yes, at age twenty and twenty-one we were both idiots.) We got on the bus and began the journey. First Bill broke out into a sweat and then his head started to sway. Then he leapt up and weaved and bumped his way down the aisle, making it to the one toilet in the back just in time. He felt sick and extremely queasy for the rest of the trip. "Thanks a lot, Jules," Bill said, sweat dripping off his brow.

Of course, I gave Bill my seat and I stood in the aisle. It was very hot, and with no air-conditioning, inside the bus it was even hotter. A handsome guy was in the seat next to Bill, a guy who eventually insisted that I sit for part of the ride. The time it took to get to London seemed interminable. Bill recovered and then flew home to Spokane, our long summer as brother and sister in Europe over. I stayed in London a few more days with the guy on the bus.

But that's another story.

So this is why we laughed together on the phone when I mentioned the souvlaki in the Pita Pit. I looked at him, through the restaurant window, in the car across the street. He was on his phone, looking back at me, his fingers on the glass of the car window. Even with the traffic on Main Street and two panes of glass between us, I could see the twinkle in his eye.

Yesterday I was able to say that my brother died yesterday.

But tomorrow I won't be able to say that. Now time is going to pull me away from him, and each day will be a day with our hands farther apart.

I'm surprised that now that Bill is dead, a new Bill is born. It's his better self, a guy I know well, who has been buried for so long inside the alcoholic. He visits me at night. I dreamed that Bill was in the middle of the pond in Manito Park, in Spokane, up to his waist. "Come on in, Jules, it's not that gross." I took a nap today on the sofa in the living room and Bill woke me up saying, "Why are you sleeping? We're gonna miss the first snow."

Bill was my constant companion growing up. We skied together almost every weekend in winter. Bill pushed me on harder and harder runs, and more runs than I wanted to take. I hear myself saying to Bill, "I'm tired, I'm hungry. Let's head back in to the lodge." I see Bill pulling out a completely smashed peanut butter and jelly half-sandwich on white bread, embalmed in Saran Wrap, and gesturing toward me, "Here, this should hold you for an hour or so."

Once, when we were adults, we went to Aspen together and he forced me down a black-diamond run, far above my ability. I cursed Bill all the way down, sidestepping with my skis for much of the way. But when he suggested we try it again, I did. It was easier. Bill would often lead me to ski jumps and then goad me over, showing me how to tuck my skis and then hustling me along before I could think of better and firmer reasons not to do it. Being with Bill was always fun. And scary.

I think of Bill with his six-pack abs, which were sadly eroded from drinking actual six-packs. But I don't want to remember that. I'm remembering him lean and taut as can be, throwing himself onto his bike. His great long, muscular legs, his unique hunch over the handlebars, his smile of enticement. "Come on, Jules. Let's go, let's go, let's go." God, his underbite—those teeth, gleaming. His ability to persevere physically seemed supernatural. He rode his bike from Spokane to Seattle several times. He hiked through the Olympic rain forest, I think more than once. He loved the early morning, and he liked to be out before anyone else, like he was stealing time.

Sadly, Bill's downhill run—the one his life was on—didn't go as well as the ones we conquered on the slopes. He was really already an alcoholic at age twenty. In his early thirties, however, he was lifted out of his chaotic vodka-fueled stupor by a strong, insightful woman, Sandy, whom he married.

He had about five good years, and fathered two amazing children, Nick and Katie. When the kids were young, he began to drink even more heavily than he had before. He became angry and cold. Sandy turned him out, and we all knew she was doing the exact right thing. Bill couldn't save himself, and if you threw him a line, he'd pull you down with him. Sandy heroically saved her children from a world of hurt. They've grown up to be resilient, thriving young adults.

Like most addicts, Bill felt deeply. He numbed himself, yes. But he also imprisoned himself in his emotions, never fully able to get beyond the sting and the heartache. He couldn't get to a perspective that was measured or thought through. He never fully moved past Michael's death—our other brother who died at age thirty-three from non-Hodgkin's lymphoma—and I could see that the alcohol and other drugs both delivered him from and kept him inside a nightmare of constant emotional pain. On the other hand he had a joyfulness about him that drew people in. He was eager and interested.

Weirdly, one of Bill's best times was when he was in jail. He was imprisoned several times for driving while drunk. Fortunately he never hurt anyone; he was just pulled over by the police for swerving all over the road. After three arrests, they sentenced him to a year.

In jail, Bill thrived. Bill needed supervision and regimentation. I had some of the best conversations with Bill when he was in prison. While a big part of his personality was a profound resistance to authority, when he was in the prison system—when it was clear there was no way out—he put his defiance aside. He followed the rules, he helped his fellow prisoners. He was assigned to the kitchen, where he was a cook. He was lucid and articulate, and he read constantly: Richard Dawkins, David Quammen, Barbara Kingsolver. I think Quammen's *Monster of God* was his most recent jail-time favorite. The last book we talked about seriously was one I sent him, *The Great Hunger* by Cecil Woodham-Smith, a book about the Irish famine. I haven't even read my own copy yet. Now we will never discuss it together.

In April, I was in Spokane and Bill was in the hospital. He had hepatitis C, kidney disease, and cirrhosis, and MRSA on top of all that. He'd also broken his wrist (which he did several times over) from falling. I stood next to his hospital bed and held his hand. He was orange from the cirrhosis—even his eyes—his stomach enlarged, and he was strapped down. Dying of alcoholism is a grisly way to go. He looked at me and said, "Hey, Jules, let's go on a hike while you're here." I held his gaze. I blinked away the tears. "Sure," I replied.

I never thought he'd leave the hospital, but he did. He seemed slightly recovered. He was walking around with a cane then, like he was a much older man.

My mother was at the end of her rope. By the time I was visiting in Spokane just last month, Bill wasn't drinking anymore, but he seemed to be declining anyway. My mother wanted him to go back in the hospital, but Bill didn't want to go. I took Bill to a doctor's appointment because of a boil he had on his neck. We sat in the waiting room for almost two hours together, reading magazines. We drove around and looked at a house we grew up in, on Twenty-sixth Street, and we gazed at the tree in front we both knew so well. We drove by our grandmother Henrietta's house on Bernard Street and noted that the shutters had been painted. This was where my aunt Barbara lived, too; she also died from alcoholism, and also turned yellow at the end.

If that seems like we knew it was good-bye to those locations, we didn't. This is what we always did when we were together in Spokane. It was our ritual.

I tried to hang out with Bill for as much of the rest of the weekend as I could. He lived in a rooming house downtown, and he had his friends. They were mostly drug addicts, recovering addicts, some very elderly, and very poor people. They had one bathroom at the end of the hallway for all of them to share. Bill introduced me to a woman, in her eighties, for whom he'd buy groceries when he could. He told me she had repaid him and accidentally written him a check for two hundred dollars, when what she owed him was only twenty dollars. He returned the check and she said she'd mixed up that check with her rent check and thanked him profusely. It was hard for me to understand how this woman came to live in a place like that room-ing house, without even a bathroom of her own. On the other hand, I found her inspiring. And frankly, this was true for the whole place. Yes, it was grimy and sad, but if you stayed there a little while, you could feel the embers of connectedness and community.

I met other friends of Bill's, people down on their luck. I was reacquainted with his friend Pete, who's a member of the Spo-kane Tribe of Native Americans. Pete told me he had a steel plate in his head and all his brothers were in jail. There was another friend in a wheelchair down the hall, who was a struggling addict. There was a couple in one room with a TV set, and other tenents crowded in watching like it was a dorm room.

The floor of Bill's room was lined with books, stacked neatly on their sides. They looked like caterpillars, crawling out of the baseboards, twisting their way up. I teased out one book from the middle of a stack and asked Bill where he found it, an early paperback edition of Will Cuppy's *The Decline and Fall of Prac-tically Everybody*. "The mission has a bin of books outside," he replied. I resisted making a joke regarding the title of the book and the place he found it. Our eyes met across the room. We laughed, not having to articulate why. We discussed *Blue Lati-tudes* by Tony Horowitz, a book I gave Bill a year or so ago. Next to that was *A Year of Magical Thinking* by Joan Didion. Bill asked me to get that book out for him. "I haven't read that one yet," he said. It seemed like an odd choice. I handed him the book and then I left for my mother's condo.

The next day Mulan flew to Spokane from O'Hare Airport, on her own. It was her first flight by herself, ever. I'd paid the "unaccompanied minor" fee and Bill and I drove out to the airport together to get her. Bill felt too weak to walk all the way to the gate, and I left him near the check-in counter and went to fetch Mulan. When we emerged from the security gates, Bill was standing there, leaning on his cane. I appreciated that Mulan gave him a big hug without me nudging her.

The next day I called Bill as soon as I woke up to see how he was feeling. He said he thought he probably should go back to Emergency. But in our family, going to Emergency often defies the word. I asked him if he wanted to go to Emergency at eleven? At noon?

Writing this now it seems so surreal, but taking Bill to Emergency was so commonplace by then, it was like another errand. Bill came to my mother's condo. He didn't eat. He said he wasn't feeling well but didn't elaborate. The boil on his neck was bigger. We all ate scrambled eggs and he sat in the living room quietly. My mother's eyes were simultaneously dilated and glazed. Another battle to save a son was about to be lost, but it wasn't a foregone conclusion yet, and Bill always seemed able to rally himself back to life.

Around noon, Mulan and I took him to the Emergency room. They admitted him right away; they knew everything about Bill. They asked us to come back with him to the area where they prepared people to enter other areas of the hospital. Mulan and I sat together on folding chairs while Bill got himself disrobed, in an area cordoned off with beige curtains for a little privacy. I have a flickering image of Bill through the partially pulled curtains, sliding off his pants and shirt to get into the gown. Now, I think about how that was the last time. His last time to pull off his pants. When I think of him sliding himself onto the hospital bed, I think about how that was his last time to slide himself onto a bed. He had an impish way about him, light on his feet, youthful even. But is that true? Maybe that's just me transforming his movements, because I knew him as a boy.

While we sat there we watched the hubbub of the emergency room. A man arrived with a bullet in his leg. He was accompanied by two policemen who may have participated in putting it there. There was a man who seemed to be having a heart attack; paddles were pulled out. A little girl arrived who'd had a terrible accident. An industrial-sized sewing needle from a large machine had been shot into her knee. She was screaming and holding a stuffed bear. Mulan's eyes were so big, just watching. "This is the real world," I said to her. Then I hated myself for saying something so trite. "Well, everything is the real world," I added. Mulan, irritated, frowned at me, like I was interrupting an absorbing TV show.

We went in and talked to Bill. The nurses had him hooked up to some fluids and were going to take him off to some other area of the hospital. We said good-bye, like it was nothing, like see you later.

I really only have feelings of sympathy for my brother Bill. He couldn't conquer this demon. Who knows what kind of fate was written for him in his genes and in his experiences? Frankly I don't think he had a choice. I don't know why some people are able to change their destructive behaviors and why some people aren't. And truthfully, I don't think anyone does.

Now, this third week I am home alone, I've been on the phone all day and night with my sister, Meg, who lives in Japan, and my brother Jim, who is with my mother in Spokane. I am on the line with my aunts, with friends who knew Bill. We're planning the funeral for August, in Spokane, when everyone is home from their summer vacations. Then my mother is going to come here and stay with me for a week or more.

My emotions roll over me like waves. I feel strong one minute, but then I am a puddle of tears the next. I am relieved—I am relieved for Bill, and relieved for his kids. No more worrying that Bill is going to show up high or drunk.

When I'm not on the phone, my mind scrambles. When I'm in yoga class, my mind hops. I'm agitated. I have very low energy.

My mother called and said that when she got Bill's backpack at the hospital after he died, she found the book *The Year of Magical Thinking*. She said she was going to read it. She said she thought Bill had left that book in there for her.

I wasn't sure she was wrong.

CHAPTER FIFTEEN

Starter Gods

I think we need a breather. I think we should talk about the death of fairy tales. But wait, I love fairy tales! Not, however, when they're presented as the truth, to a little child who doesn't have the critical thinking skills to be appropriately skeptical. On the other hand, I love to pretend, I love fantasy, I love imagining. This has been the bread and butter of my career. But here's the thing: I know I am fantasizing when I'm fantasizing.

You see, I went through a rather rigorous philosophical upheaval shortly before I became a mother and this caused me to feel very deeply that I should absolutely never lie to Mulan. I felt I had been deliberately lied to as a child, and I resented it. And even though my struggle had to do with religion, it bled out from there. To Santa Claus, for example.

When I thought about Santa Claus in the abstract—the myth's connection to my own childhood, and the joy of the festive images and the presents and the tree and all the folklore—it was great. It was a part of the seasonal fun of being a parent and being a kid.

But when it came to the reality of it, to what you had to do to create that magical mystery, I balked. I felt incapable of peering into Mulan's sweet, open, naïve, trusting eyes and lying to her. I was her protector and overseer, and this rankled me deeply. I just couldn't do it.

Since Mulan was only two for her first Christmas with me, it was easy to just skip it all. When she was three, Santa Claus was around but he was just art. His cheerful image was on things, but I didn't feel compelled to explain him. And she wasn't in school yet, so I didn't have to deal with other kids' expectations and assumptions, either.

By the time Mulan turned four, however, I had changed my mind. I felt I was cheating her out of a great holiday tradition and this wonderful feeling of magic and the remarkable characters and stories of her culture. I mean, c'mon, it was fun. Why was I such a stick in the mud?

I didn't realize that it was actually kind of late to introduce a kid to the concept of Santa Claus. At this age, she was already a person with some critical thinking skills and when I began to tell her about Santa, I just ended up scaring the hell out of her.

Because I had dithered in my mind about how to say it, I delayed, and didn't end up telling her about Santa until Christmas Eve. That year we were alone, just the two of us, in Los Angeles. We had a tree, and a few presents. But I had kept most of her gifts hidden in a closet so that "Santa Claus" could bring them out.

So, just before she went to bed, I said, "I need to tell you something. There is this guy . . . his name is Santa Claus and he, well, frankly he's been watching you."

She looked terrified.

Maybe that wasn't the best way to begin.

She asked, "When?"

I said, "He . . . he can see you all the time. He is sort of like, invisible and he can watch you and he knows if you've been a good girl or not."

Her face showed deep concern. She said, "Yeah. . . ."

I said, "And well . . . he—based on your behavior over the last year, which in my opinion has been pretty good—well, based on that, he is going to come in our house tonight, while we're asleep, and bring you some presents and put them under our tree."

"What?" Mulan cried.

"I know," I said.

"How is he going to get in our house?" she asked.

"Well, he actually . . . he comes down the chimney—y'know, through the fireplace."

"What? Why? Why doesn't he just come through the door?"

"Because . . . because he's magic?" I smiled and shrugged.

"So," Mulan stated flatly.

"Well, it's his traditional way, because he's magic, and. . . ."

"But if he's magic, he could just make the presents appear there, under the tree."

"I know, that's a good point, it's, it's . . . just his way," I scrambled.

Mulan's face filled with terror thinking about this. She actually began to shake. "I'm not sleeping alone tonight!" she cried.

I ended up letting her sleep with me. She had a hard time falling asleep and every sound made her wake and grab for me in fear. There was nothing about it that was fun or good or, least of all, magical. It was all just horrible.

In the morning, while she was still asleep, I put the presents under the tree. I came into the bedroom and gently woke her. I said, "Let's go in the living room and see if Santa Claus came!"

She sucked in a loud and fearful gulp of air. "No!" she yelled. "Mommy, no!" I had to lift her out of the bed, kicking and screaming. I had never seen her so afraid and deeply disturbed.

The point is: I didn't do a very good job with Santa Claus.

Maybe because I felt like such a failure in this department, I began to resent the whole idea of Santa Claus even more. It became so obvious to me that Santa was just a starter god. It was a way to ease a kid into an idea that was to be taken even more seriously later. Think about it: "He knows if you've been bad or good, so be good for *goodness* sake?" He even looks like the traditional Western image of God, the white hair, the white beard.

On the other hand, I didn't want to turn into a curmudgeon (although it might be too late for that).

Even so, I kept things up for the next two years. At six, Mulan lost a tooth and I realized I was going to have to go through all of this again with the Tooth Fairy. This, too, traumatized Mulan. I explained calmly, "There's this woman, and if you leave your tooth under your pillow during the night, while you're sleeping, she will come and take it and leave you money."

"What?" Mulan's eyes bugged out.

"Yes."

Mulan looked at the tooth in her hand, her prized possession. "What does she want the teeth for?" Mulan asked.

"Well . . . she . . . she . . . I don't know exactly; she just wants them and she's willing to pay for them."

"She takes the tooth from under my pillow? While I'm asleep?"

I could see where we were headed.

"She's very small, she's a fairy—a teeny fairy, and she's going to fly in, by magic—"

"Like a wasp?"

I resisted the impulse to say, "No, she's actually a Catholic."

"Well, how much . . . how much does she give you for your tooth?" Mulan looked at her tooth like she didn't know if she was willing to part with it.

"I don't know, fifty cents maybe."

"Fifty cents," Mulan said skeptically. She scrunched up her nose suggesting the question, What can you get for fifty cents?

"Or a dollar even." I was upping the price, I hadn't accounted for inflation. I couldn't remember what I had gotten. The Tooth Fairy idea was not going over well.

"I don't want anyone flying into my room and going under

my pillow," Mulan stated with reason. "If a fairy is coming into my room tonight and going under my pillow, well, that's scary. So, I'll do it, but I want to sleep with you."

Ah . . . Mulan was always very good at leveraging new information into a bargain for what she really wanted.

It occurred to me that if Santa Claus was a starter god in general, the Tooth Fairy was the starter god of capitalism. You have something, and someone else wants it. It may be something that you find completely useless, although it has value to someone else.

So, she did put the tooth under her pillow, but she slept with me and we both went into her room together in the morning to see what had transpired overnight.

A year or so later, I was sitting in a chair reading the paper and Mulan walked up to me with her hands deliberately behind her back. She said, "What is this?" When she said the word "this" she dramatically revealed a Baggie she'd been hiding behind her back, and waved it in front of my nose.

I had saved her teeth. I felt odd throwing them away. I figured maybe we'd make earrings out of them, or buttons for a doll's dress. I don't know, something. But at this moment I felt I was on a witness stand. "It appears to be a plastic bag with some small teeth in it." I stammered.

"Mom, are you the Tooth Fairy?"

"Yes," I said. I wondered for a moment if she thought I was everyone's Tooth Fairy, the world's Tooth Fairy, but she didn't.

Mulan went on: "You're the one who took my teeth and gave me the money."

"Yes. I did."

"Are you Santa Claus?"

"Yes. I am."

She seemed very proud of herself and I was relieved. I was glad all this nonsense was over.

But it wasn't.

When the next Christmas arrived, Mulan asked, "What if I believe in Santa? If I believe in him, then isn't he real?"

"Not really," I said. "But if you want to believe in Santa, go right ahead."

It was a little awkward. She started saying things like, "Oh, I hope Santa knows how good I am!" She wrote a letter to Santa and wanted to actually mail it. I went along with all of it. I felt a little creepy, like we were an old, bored married couple who had to dress up in outfits to spice things up. I pretended with her, but I was gulping back reluctance and grimacing. I kept trying to get myself going, thinking, This is up my alley, I'm an actress, let's just go for it. But I don't think I was all that convincing.

But then I realized that she also wanted to reenact finding out that Santa was not real, too. We would drive around town and she'd say, "How can those reindeer fly?" I would come up with some semi-believable-sounding answer that we both knew was fabricated.

Finally I got sick of it, and one day when she asked, "I mean, how can Santa, who is so fat, fit down the chimney?" I said, "Look, Mulan. If you want to believe in Santa, go ahead. But I think it's a little like believing in God. You just have to do it and not ask a lot of questions. Otherwise you won't be able to do it."

"Oh," she said. "That's not that fun."

"See, I don't want you to believe in something that doesn't

make sense. So I have no incentive to keep answering these questions. Find someone who wants you to believe in Santa Claus and ask that person all your questions."

"Like who?" Mulan asked.

"Well, how about Grandma?" I said, smiling.

CHAPTER SIXTEEN

Pussy

This is a story about two terminated pregnancies. I suppose I am surrendering certain moral ground by including this story in the death section of my book. But, like the pregnancies, the "Death Week" of this book was not planned.

Here's why I want to include it: to me being a mother is something that, thanks to science, women can choose to be or not. Choosing to be a mother implicitly implies another choice, a choice not to be a mother. These choices are significant, too. People don't talk about them enough. As I write this, the right to a safe, legal abortion is part of the political discussion, and a woman's right to have this option available to her is gradually being taken away in many of the United States.

When my mother-in-law, Norma, and I decided to talk about parenting and record our conversation, I had no idea where the conversation would go. I didn't expect to be sharing abortion stories. In any case, the discussion went where it went and I'm glad about that. Norma is eighty-five and now resides in my bungalow in Hollywood. She visits us in Wilmette regularly.

Norma divorced Michael's father, Al (who is now deceased), more than thirty years ago. She lived in Washington, D.C., for thirty-five years, and before that she and Al and their two boys lived in various places, including New York, New Jersey, Florida, California, and Mexico. She and Al met in Brooklyn, where Norma had grown up.

My mother married when she was twenty-one and had me by the time she was twenty-two. She had five children. My mother is a practicing Catholic, as was my father. She expected and wanted to have many children, and birth control was not something openly talked about.

Norma got married at twenty-one as well, but she didn't have her first son—my husband—until she was twenty-eight.

Here is a transcript of a part of our conversation. (It's smoothed out somewhat for clarity.)

Julia: Tell me about how you didn't expect to have kids when you first got married. Were you going to use birth control?

Norma: Well, when we first met each other, my husband told me he was sterile. But I'd heard that from other boys!

Julia: Why would someone say that?

Norma: Because they want to get in your pants. And we didn't have really good birth control. Some girls had diaphragms. Most people did not have birth control, and yeah, I believed him. What did I know? I just sat there looking really sophisticated. If you'd seen me! But I knew nothing, really. I always looked, acted, like I knew so much, when really—I knew nothing. You know, in fourth grade, Charles Haracletis said to me, "Norma, you know everything. How does it happen?" I said, "What do you want to know?" And he said, "When a man pees up a woman, is that fucking?" Ha! In fourth grade! I said, "Oh Charles, what a childish question." But the truth was, I had no idea. I *had* to tell my mother when I got home. My mother had a great laugh, and you could never tell about my mother, whether she was going to slap you for being insolent, or she was going to burst out laughing. But in this case, she laughed. Anyway, that's what Al told me; he thought he was sterile. I didn't question it. This fit into my plans exactly because I was going to be a career woman. My father encouraged that. After a while, I figured out that Al probably wasn't sterile and I started using birth control, although I was very haphazard and lazy about it. It was all sort of vague. So there you are. Things don't always work out the way you expect, but look at the luck.

Julia: So how long were you married before you had Michael?

Norma: Almost seven years. But Al and I were together for two years before we got married.

Julia: What year did you get married?

Norma: 1949. Michael was born in 1955.

Julia: When you first got pregnant, how did you feel about it?

Norma: I couldn't believe it. We were living in the country then, in the woods in New Jersey. When my doctor told me I was pregnant, I got really upset. My doctor said, "What's the matter?" I said, "Well, I'm too young." My doctor said, "Don't be ridiculous. You're too *old*." And that was true for that part of the world. When I had Michael, I was the oldest first-time mother in the maternity ward. There were two women in each room, and a common area with a couch and a coffee machine. Being in a maternity ward was an incredible experience because you would tell the person in the next bed things about yourself you really wouldn't tell your best friend. And they're telling you the same thing. You know, "My husband's penis is too big." You'd hear things like that; it was incredible. I shared my room with two girls—the first one was there when I got there, and halfway through she left and I spent the last half with another woman. The first one was twenty years old and she was having her fourth kid. She'd gotten married when she was fifteen; she'd gotten pregnant and ran off with her boyfriend to get married. She had her first baby when she was fifteen and a half. Her oldest child, a boy, would come in during visiting hours. He had a little sailor hat. It was . . . honestly, it was really weird. My next roommate was a woman who was in her forties and just had twins. Her oldest child, a daughter, was twenty-two years old. And this poor kid was humiliated that her mother was giving birth, because she was so old. Not only that, her father—the husband of the woman with the twins—had just left her for a younger woman. So this meant this woman was facing raising these twins by herself. I'll never forget the last thing I heard the daughter say to her mother about the babies. She said, "Don't worry mother, we'll get used to it." *We'll get used to it.* With such sad resignation.

Well, a little while after I had Michael I realized I hadn't gotten my period in a couple of months. I was pregnant again less than a year later with Joel. My maternity clothes were still hanging on the back of my chair.

Julia: How did Al handle having the kids?

Norma: He was happy enough; he was crazy about the two kids, and he felt like that was a whole family. And I did, too. But Julia, I was overwhelmed with two babies in diapers. I also had four dogs and two cats! And I sort of had a job, very part-time, but still. A lot to deal with. And I was naturally incompetent at things like diapers and formula and managing everything. By then we'd moved to Washington, D.C. I was working for a publisher part-time, editing.

So when I got pregnant a third time I was extremely upset and very, very worried. I decided I would get an abortion. Al didn't dissuade me. You know, women who say there is nothing to getting an abortion. I'm here to attest to you, it's not nothing. It's something.

Julia: Tell me. Tell me.

Norma: So there I was pregnant again, the third time. I had a friend named Murray, who was an optometrist—and he was a connector-type person, he knew everybody and who everybody knew. And he was a very energetic, friendly guy. I mentioned to him that I thought I was pregnant, and I said meaningfully, "Do you know somebody?" He said, "No! What are you talking about? Know who?" We had a funny relationship, me and Murray, I said to him, "No, Murray, it's 'know whom.' " And that was the end of the conversation.

Two days later my phone rang, and this woman said, "My name is Tippy. Meet me in the lobby of the Wood-ner Hotel with two hundred dollars in cash and I will explain to you how we can solve your problem." I said, "How will I know you?" She said, "I'll know you . . . and I'll be wearing a mink coat." A mink coat! That made me laugh. It's all such a sad memory, but also funny. Al came with me to meet Tippy. It was a big deal. We were meet-ing her after nine o'clock at night; we had to get a baby-sitter. There was Tippy, all of twenty-two years old, and wearing a mink coat. I'll never forget her. We sat down and ordered drinks. She took the two hundred dollars and said to us, "You're going to go for a pre-exam." She took out a piece of paper and said, "Look at it, memorize this address." There was no telephone number, no name, just an address. She wouldn't let us write it down. Then she said, "They'll tell you whether they'll take you or not. If they do, you'll give them nine hundred dollars." Al asked, "Can we pay with a check?" She rolled her eyes and said, "No! It has to be in cash." And then, I know this is a small detail, but when the bill came, Tippy handed it to us, so *we* could pay for the drinks.

Julia: Ha, ha. That's not a small detail, I'd never forget that part, either.

Norma: I've never forgotten any of it.

Julia: But Norma, that's so much money, eleven hundred dollars. In 1960.

Norma: Yes, it was a lot of money.

Julia: Why did they not know if they would take you or not?

Norma: Because if you were after a certain time along, they wouldn't take you.

Julia: So, what happened?

Norma: Well, we went to this address. It was on a Monday at five-thirty P.M. You know, Washington is encircled by suburbs that tell you who you are and where you are. And this is one of those 1950s suburbs. . . . It's not poverty stricken by any means. It was certainly not a slum. But it was depressing beyond belief: the houses are all alike and small, and there are chain link fences. It was hard to find this house, at first. But then we did find it—it was painted bright green with black shutters. We rang the bell and waited a really long time. A voice finally said, "Just a minute." We waited longer. Finally the door opened and it was very dim inside, and decorated unlike the outside would lead you to expect—dark red with all these Oriental artifacts, lots of junk everywhere. There were hardly any lights on. A voice told us to come in further. We went in further. There stood this little guy, who looked just like Murray—he wasn't Murray, of course, but he was short and wiry just like him. He said to me, "Pull up your skirt."

Julia: What?

Norma: Yes, he says, "Pull up your skirt." And I *did*. He felt around, which was—

Julia: Creepy!

Norma: Yes, very creepy. Then he said, "Yeah, you're okay." He went to a desk and picked up the phone and said to someone, "Hello, I have a delivery of *snow tires*. What date can you pick them up?" (For years after this, whenever I heard the words "snow tires" I thought of this moment.) Anyway, he got off the phone and said, "Go to this corner in Baltimore." You know like on Wednesday at ten-thirty A.M. He showed us a piece of paper with the address. We gave him the nine hundred dollars and then he said to Al in a very brusque voice, "Don't try to talk to the driver, and do not try to follow him and see where he's going. He'll bring your wife back to the exact same corner five hours later." Then he said to me, "You will

170

wait at the corner, and so they know who you are, you should carry a *Reader's Digest.*" And what do you think I said to him?

Julia: Knowing you, Norma, it was that you weren't going to carry a *Reader's Digest.*

Norma: Yes! You're right! That part was putting me over the edge.

Julia: Oh God!

Norma: I almost called the whole thing off right there. I said, "I agree to it all, but I'll be carrying a *Harper's.*"

Julia: Oh my God. Norma, I can't believe you had to go through this.

Norma: Oh, there's so much more. So we did go to this corner. Al had the kids in the car, we had a camp wagon then, and the two kids were in the back with their toys, I was crying in the front of the car, I was getting so worried. I was worked up and distraught.

Julia: Oh, Norma.

Norma: I got out of the van with my *Harper's.* In a little while, a large black sedan drove up. And Julia, it was driven by Pussy, from *The Sopranos.* Of course, I didn't know he was Pussy until I watched *The Sopranos,* but when I saw him on that show, I said to myself—I know that guy! He looked exactly like this guy who drove this car. Anyway, I get in the car. There were already two other women in the backseat, and they were blindfolded.

Julia: What?

Norma: Yes, he had blindfolded them! Pussy handed me a blindfold and said, "Put it on." I did. We picked up two more women, so eventually we were five women, all blindfolded, in this car. The windows were all dark, so no one could look in.

Julia: Weren't you scared?

Norma: Well, yes, I was terrified. I was so worried, what if I was orphaning my kids because I was having an abortion? I was so scared. I was out of my mind with fear. But, to be honest with you, I was also titillated. I already couldn't wait to tell Al about it, because I knew I could never tell anyone else about this, ever. Not even my best friend. We drove for about an hour, and then the car stopped and Pussy let us take the blindfolds off. We were in an alley. But saying an alley, it makes it seem dark and sinister, but it wasn't at all. It was an alley that was well lit and used by all the people who lived on this street to drive into their garages, just like you have now. We went into this house through the back door. We were taken into the living room, which was very small, and had five uncomfortable chairs. We all sat down and for the first time I looked at the other women, and we were such a motley assortment. One was older, she looked fifty! And one woman cried, sobbed, the entire time.

Then, while we were sitting there waiting for our turn, this two-and-a-half-year-old baby of great adorability was wandering around saying, "Mama, Mama!" He belonged to the woman who owned the house. He was her kid, wandering around; so painful and surreal. We just sat there in silence, just the kid saying "Mama" and the one woman sobbing into her handkerchief. Some of us began talking to each other. The woman crying was forty-four, and she was in a relationship with a guy. They weren't married and he didn't want to have kids with her. She was too afraid to raise a child all by herself, but she was in anguish, because from her point of view it was her last chance to have a baby.

They beckoned us, one by one. They called my name and I went upstairs. A nurse in a starched uniform handed me a gown. She said, "Go in there, take your clothes off; the opening of the gown is in front." All the furniture had been taken out of one of the upstairs bedrooms, and it was made up like an operating room. The doctor said, "Lay down." They gave you a mild anesthetic. I spread my legs and in two seconds, it was over. I was sort of sleepy. They took me to another room where I could lie down and rest.

Then Pussy came and collected the five of us. We headed back into the city, but there was a lot of traffic, and by the time I got dropped off at my corner, many more than five hours had passed since I'd been picked up. Al wasn't there. It turned out he was just driving around the block, over and over again, like forty times. And he was a wreck, he was in a real state—weeping. He said he was worried I was dead. He said, "I kept thinking how am I going to explain to her parents how she died? That she'd been dumped somewhere?"

So, the point is, it was a horrible experience. It was unnecessarily traumatic, and not only for me, but for the other women, too. And there's the class aspect, too— every one of those people, none of them looked like they could spare eleven hundred dollars. Even though this was a high-end abortion—this was about as good as you could get. Think of all the abortions performed on really poor women—the circumstances. I am, and have always been, a vociferous defender of the right to terminate a pregnancy. If having a kid doesn't fit into your scheme of things, it doesn't matter why, even if it means you can't buy two lipsticks a week like you want to, I believe in a woman's right to do what she wants with her body. No explanations needed. On the other hand, when emancipated women say to each other, "Oh there's nothing to it," that's not right, either. There's something to it. There's a lot to it. But here's the thing, Murray never mentioned it to me again and we were friends forever. He just died two years ago. We remained friends for years, and we never mentioned it. Once I made a joke with him, like, "Do you ever hear from Tippy?" And he looked me right in the eye and said, "Tippy who?"

Julia: Wow. Wow.

Norma: In fact, back then, I *did* learn a little more about Tippy. I came to realize that she worked as a dental hygienist, in the same big building as Murray. A dental hygienist, but with a mink coat.

Julia: Ha! God, what a complicated scheme.

Norma: Oh, there's more. Afterwards, I developed an infection; I wasn't getting better in the way you should. I had a very high fever. When I left the abortionist's house, the doctor said, "You can't get in touch with any of us ever again, but if you have a problem, call this number." It was a number in another state, like Ohio, I think. One night, I was really bad, I had a fever. At three in the morning, Al did call the number. Some guy said to him, "What's the nearest twenty-four-hour pharmacy near your house?" Al told him about one just down the street. And Al went there and got some antibiotic that this Ohio doctor had called in.

Julia: Wow. What a harrowing story. I can't believe you had to go through it.

Norma: A lot of women did this.

Julia: Well, I had an abortion, too. And I was also married when I had it.

Norma: In Los Angeles?

Julia: Yes. It was in Los Angeles. There were two things that made having the baby impossible. The biggest one that trumped everything was that we didn't have the money to have a child. We were both starting out in highly precarious careers. Secondly, I was feeling ambivalent about the marriage itself. On top of all of this, I was in the middle of rehearsals for a play. So, when I found I was pregnant and I told my husband I was going to get an abortion, he didn't object. I wanted to take care of the whole business myself, and not involve him.

Looking back, I think I may have been afraid that the abortion itself would bring us closer together emotionally. I was worried that I would feel pressure to be emotional about it when I just wanted to be done with the procedure. I didn't want to cry with him. I wanted to cry by myself. Looking back on it now, I feel sad for me, because it is another example of me going my own individual way and refusing help. But in the long run, I understand why I felt this way, because this marriage was not working, and I knew it.

Norma: Where did you have the abortion?

Julia: I drove myself to East L.A., to this clinic, and I went alone. I had to pay three hundred and twenty dollars, in cash. I went in and they tested me for my pregnancy and I went in this room and I put all my clothes in a locker and then put on a gown. Then I had to sit on these long locker benches, filled with women. It was like an abortion assembly line. They took in four women at a time. When the next group of women went into the operating room, we all moved down the long bench. I wasn't feeling conflicted about this decision, but when I got close to the door, I began to cry really hard. I wasn't really crying for me, either, but for the whole situation, for all these women, for all these women who were making this big decision. It was like you could feel how big a deal this was for everyone, and everyone's lives were going to be forever changed when they left, and none of us were going to forget about it, ever.

There was a woman next to me, she was Hispanic, and older. She had a Mexican accent. She said, "Do you have children?" And I said, "No. But I just can't." She patted my back and said, "You do what you need to do." And then she said, "I have four children already. I can't." Then she comforted me and hugged me. That was the most astonishing thing of all—she comforted *me,* this woman with four children. I'll never forget her. The abortion itself, as you said, too, was nothing at all.

Afterward, I had to lie and tell them I had someone to drive me home. I parked my car a couple of blocks away so no one who worked there could see me get in the driver's seat. I came home and I felt a little sick. I had cramps. But I went to a play practice that night—I went to rehearsal. I couldn't miss that. Mostly, though, I felt very heroic. The thing is, that abortion was really a turning point for me. The unexpected feelings I had about it weren't loss or regret or guilt, feelings I anticipated to wash over me. I was surprised to feel deeply empowered. I knew I had to get out of that marriage. I knew I wanted to do so many things, and go so many places. By myself. My abortion made me feel that I had control over my future. I wasn't going to just let certain things happen to me. Soon after this my husband and I did split up. He went on to marry a beautiful woman and have three lovely children. He is actually a very nice guy. But our situation was not the right one for me.

Norma: I can't believe we're even talking about abortion in politics right now. This is really a sign of our lunacy. I have to tell you, your experience might have had its poignant side, but at least it was legal. You didn't have to get into a big black car with a gangster and be blindfolded. Your experience seems quite normal, and ordinary and not fraught with this kind of encompassing drama that really could take over your life. You know, sometimes I get in bed and these images come up in my head. It's something to live with that. As long as women like me are still alive, there will be stories to tell that are just like my story.

Julia: That's true. Let's hope it stays legal.

Norma: The sad truth is, wealthy women have only the children they want to have. They will always be able to get an abortion if they want one, and relatively speaking, all of us women, those five women getting the abortion with me, in 1960, they were wealthy compared with the general population. So if it becomes illegal it will only be the poor women who won't be able to get an abortion, because the wealthy will always have a way. And those poorer women are exactly the women who need to have that choice the most.

CHAPTER SEVENTEEN

Baby on Board

I have a minivan, a Honda Odyssey. I told you already that I loved my minivan. But let me tell you more about why. I can easily take eight people anywhere; I can carry a dresser and a double-bed mattress if I need to. I can drop off several children after a sleepover with all their gear, and we can travel up to Door County in Wisconsin to camp with all our equipment and a dog and even bikes and everyone is comfortable.

Yes, it's a big car. Yes, I've written adamantly about the obnoxiousness of big strollers. So you could say I'm full of it. But I've moved to a place that accommodates big cars. When I took

Mulan to her first gymnastics class at the Wilmette Recreation Center, I pulled into the parking lot and was stunned, momentarily overcome with emotion. There were so many parking spaces! I said to Mulan, as I got choked up with tears, "Look, I could park here. Or over there. Or over there. I can choose!" At Mulan's gymnastics venue in L.A.—ten miles from our house—forty-five minutes each way in traffic—we had to wait in a line to valet park our car. Then the attendants parked the cars in tandem, adding much time and expense after each class.

The best thing of all about being here, however, is that I barely drive. Maybe fifty miles a week, at most. Everything is less than two miles away. In Los Angeles I was driving three hundred miles a week on average. So yes, I have a big minivan. But mostly it sits and waits for me to drive three blocks to the grocery store. So don't give me those looks, you people who live in big cities and drive Priuses. In the environmental transportation wars, I win.

On the other hand, I do not live in a cool, hip place. I do not get to be astounded very often at the style and flair of a random person walking down the street. I don't get to be surrounded by the urban mix, the entrancing graffiti, the sense of many peoples of many backgrounds converging in the talky, energetic soup of a big city. Mostly what I see are women pushing strollers. Leading the way as a couple of more kids walk behind. The entire city of Wilmette is set up to accommodate families. While I appreciate this, it can be mind-numbing. Also, I should add that I live in the city of blond ponytails; one might describe it as a sea of blond ponytails. It's practically the required hairstyle of the town. Truth be told, after a year here, I realized that the blond ponytails were not all the same, as the distinctions among the blonds revealed themselves: strawberry, platinum, dishwater, sandy, ash. And the placement varied, too: up, high, low, off to one side. (Okay, I admit it, I'm jealous of women with thick long hair. If I could have a ponytail, I would.)

On the other hand, Evanston, less than a mile from us, is a university town where many of the shop clerks have dreadlocks and everyone is tattooed and super-groovy. I describe to my Los Angeles friends that residing here is like living in Logan, Utah, six blocks from Berkeley, California.

But I'd like to put all this aside now, and discuss something related to cars and children. I would like to describe some of the driving dramas Mulan and I have had.

Recently, Mulan and I had one of our worst fights. She was riding in the front seat, had tossed off her shoes, and was resting her bare feet on the dash. She was texting her friends but also looking up from time to time to ask why I hadn't turned at this or that street. I used to have many discussions with Mulan about "tone." Tone is a very important concept. The same words can have a million different meanings based on what tone is used. I taught her that in Cantonese (the language of her people) there are seven different "tones." (Yes, I know I'm mixing up the definitions of the word. And I'm sure Noam Chomsky would have a heart attack over how I'm conflating attitudinal tone with phonological tone, but uh . . . suck it Chomsky.)

The reason I bring up tone in this story is that I felt Mulan's body language was expressing an overly casual and superior "tone." I realized in that moment that not only language can have a "tone"; bodies can as well. And I didn't like hers right then.

181

We got to her piano lesson and there were, uncharacteristically, no parking spaces in front. Mulan insisted that I could get into one particular parking space that I didn't want to try because it looked too small. Finally I got really angry and basically stopped the car in front of the building and yelled, "Get out! Get out!" A student (Mulan takes piano on the Northwestern University campus) who was walking by turned to look at me. Mulan grabbed her piano books and bolted, while making an exasperated, angry sound, conveying a frustrated and dismissive tone.

Caught by the student, I turned red. *Angry mommy yelling at daughter.* Shit, I had to pull myself together.

Our troubles in the car go way back. In fact, Mulan was a backseat driver even when she was a baby, in her car seat.

First, I must tell you about the seating configuration in my former car. I put the car seat in the backseat near the right passenger door. It made it easiest to get Mulan in the car, and when I was driving I could turn my head to the right and see her.

One day, when Mulan was about three, I was driving and suddenly noticed a sound, a sound like a window was open. In the split second I had before I could see what was really happening, I had a thought: Oh, she's figured out how to open the electric window. But when I actually did turn to look, I could see that she had not learned how to open the electric window. She had learned how to open the car door. In fact, she was leaning out of her car seat and watching the pavement slide by beneath her arm, which had thrust the car door open. Her left leg was splayed out toward me as if she might voluntarily dive into the street. She exhibited no fear, only fascination.

It looked like she could topple out of her car seat at any moment and I would have driven over her. Looking back, she was probably securely strapped into the car seat and the car seat was strapped into the car. But still.

My heart nearly squeezed out of my eyeballs. I immediately pulled over and closed her door. Of course, I began to use the childproof locks. Duh. But then, having had the thrill once, Mulan would just pull the latch to open the door and let it flick back into place with a *thwack*. Over and over. Over and over. Over and over into mother madness.

I decided to move her car seat to the middle of the backseat. Away from both windows. But while my car didn't have bucket seats (are there bucket seats anymore?), it did have a little hump in the middle of the backseat. This is important because it put Mulan in a subtle but significant new position. She was now sitting up, an inch or two higher than she had been before. In fact, if I looked into the rearview mirror, I saw only her smiling face. I had to reposition the rearview mirror. Now that Mulan's head was a bit higher in the car, relative to mine, she began to look out the windshield. She began to look a bit like Carl Sagan in the series *Cosmos*. It was funny; it made me laugh. Big Baby Head coming down the road.

But after a while I wasn't laughing anymore, because Mulan suddenly had a lot of opinions about my driving. "Why are you in this lane?" she would say, age four or four and a half, her big godhead looking out and surveying the land. "Why don't you get into the right lane and pass? No one's in the right lane; just get over there."

"Mom, why did you take a left? We don't usually go this way."

"There was a parking space, Mom. You missed it!"

"You better get gas soon; we're running a little low."

All from her goddamned car seat. When Mulan was about five, I was telling a friend about this, and Mulan overheard us. I said, "She's a backseat driver, from the car seat!" Mulan came in and said, "Mom, I know what a backseat driver is, but why do you add 'from a car seat' to it? Why is that important?" I said, "Because you are a little kid, a little kid so small that you require sitting in a car seat."

"Oh, I get it," she said. "But why is that funny?"

"Because people wouldn't think that such a little kid, a kid in a car seat, would have so many opinions about how her mother was driving! Because she is essentially a baby, and does not drive."

"Oh," Mulan said. "Now I get it. Funny." She was not smiling. I think she was mimicking me. Comedians don't usually laugh at each other; we just label something "funny," and Mulan had picked up on that.

But I could tell that her tone was slightly condescending.

CHAPTER EIGHTEEN

The Color of Skin

Why am I including this essay in here? I suppose it's because it's about the death of innocence. Except it's also about innocence regained (or maintained) in an odd way, through distraction and obliviousness, two states of mind that are often maligned. (But without which we'd all be much worse off.) I'll explain.

In first grade, Mulan's class began to learn about Martin Luther King Jr.

I never brought up the idea of race with Mulan. I suppose I figured I would discuss it with her when I had something to say to her about it. But up to age six, there was never an opportunity. Frankly, it wasn't on my radar in any way.

Some people claim that our racial prejudices are innate, and that accepting people who look different requires learning tolerance and acceptance. Maybe that's true if you're raised in an environment that's dominated by one race, and it's a shock to see someone who looks unlike the established in-group. But Mulan had gone to a public school that was very racially diverse. In fact, there were days when I nearly laughed out loud as I walked into the play yard to pick her up from school: the California sunshine streaming down on an idyllic landscape of nearly equal numbers of light-skinned to very dark-skinned children all laughing together as if they were posing for an ad about the melting pot of America.

In fact, at Mulan's school, Caucasians were in the minority. I never mentioned it to her, because I barely registered it myself. There were times when her lack of awareness about race was touching—as if she were truly color-blind. If Mulan was telling me about a friend at school and I asked her to describe this friend, she would say, "Sarah—she has black curly hair and wears a lot of red?" Only when I met the friend would I know that she was black.

Once when Mulan and I were talking about a group of triplets she knew at school and sometimes played with, I said, "You know, the triplets are also from China and—" Mulan stopped me and said, "The triplets are *adopted*?" The fact that the triplets' parents were both extremely blond and fair-skinned made this more poignant (and funnier) to me. I knew that eventually

Mulan would notice these things, but I enjoyed that she was living in a Garden of Eden when it came to race.

Naturally my ears perked up when Mulan said her class was going to learn about Martin Luther King Jr. to get ready for the holiday. One evening, I was washing dishes at the sink, getting Mulan to tell me about her day at school. She stood next to me and said, "Mom, did you know that in the past, people who have really dark skin, who are called 'black people,' were slaves?"

"Yes, I did know that," I said.

"Did you know that even today some people don't like people who have dark skin?"

"Yes, I did know that," I said, "Isn't that sad—"

Mulan suddenly thrust her arm toward my face. "Mom! Look!" she said, pointing dramatically toward the middle of her forearm. "My skin is kind of dark!"

"Yes, I see that," I said. "Skin color doesn't mean anything good or bad."

"To a lot of people, it does. Some people have been killed because of their skin color!"

"Yes. That's true," I said. "Which is really wrong and sad."

"I'm just so glad I'm not black!" Mulan announced.

Oh God, I realized Mulan was learning to be racist by learning about racism. Not what her teachers intended, probably.

"That was true in the past, that a lot of black people were slaves," I started, scrambling to figure out what exactly to say. "Things are better now, although not completely, and other groups of people who happen to have darker-colored skin have been discriminated against, too. Things are getting better and the most important thing to understand is that while some people may think this way, it's not right. Skin color is just skin color, like the color of your eyes or the color of your dress or the color of an apple. It has nothing to do with better or worse; it's just skin color."

"Sarah's black, and I'm almost as dark as Sarah," Mulan said gravely.

"So what?" I said. "It's just the color your skin is."

"But not everyone feels like you do," Mulan said.

"Yes," I said. "That's true."

I realized I was handling this terribly. I had to acknowledge her fear. I couldn't downplay it. I said, "That must feel scary to think that because of something that means nothing and something you have no control over, that would make other people think things about you . . . automatically . . . that are probably not true. Plus, we live in a place where race matters very little, except when it does." Involuntarily I made a face. "And then it *really* does." At this point, I stopped talking, because I was still making things worse.

Mulan asked, "If I'm Asian, what are you?"

"I'm Caucasian," I said.

"Cock Asian?" Mulan asked, adding, "Like Asian, but also Cock?" She did not know that *cock* is a synonym for penis, so it made for hilariously uncomfortable moments when Mulan would occasionally announce to me, "I'm Asian and you're Cock Asian."

While I didn't think Mulan was experiencing any racism, I did notice a kind of reverse racism. I cannot tell you how many times people have said, before knowing anything about Mulan other than the fact that she's Chinese, that she must be really smart. This happens all the time. It puts me in this awkward position of replying, "Well, she's kind of smart. I mean she's average. She's just an average person."

I tried to steer Mulan away from stereotypical Asian girl areas of specialization. When she was five she began to ask for a violin. A girl at her school had played "Twinkle, Twinkle, Little Star" and it had sparked something in Mulan. I got her a violin. Then she began to excel in gymnastics. Then she began to be very good at math.

It embarrassed me when people asked Mulan what she liked to do and she would answer: "Violin, math, and gymnastics." I would quickly add: "And other things, too: movies, TV, jumping rope, eating tortellini!" People would smile and say, "Of course you like violin, math, and gymnastics." And then they would look at me like, "Why can't you just accept your own daughter for who she is?"

When Mulan was in second grade we went to Hawaii for a week. She and I got some plastic water toys and spent whole days in the water. Mulan's skin immediately started to get very dark in the sun. She looked gorgeous, like her skin was drinking up the rays. After seven days she was at least as dark-skinned as many people who are black.

One day soon after we returned I was on the playground, watching Mulan emerge from the class at the end of the day, talking and laughing with some friends before she headed over to me. As I watched her, a Korean mother came up to me and said, "You know, we don't let our kids get that dark."

"What?" I sputtered. I began to talk uncontrollably and skittishly: "Uh . . . we were just in Hawaii, and you know I recently had a conversation with a dermatologist who was telling me how ridiculous it is for people who have darker skin tones to fear skin cancer, and that like—it's only the people like me, who have this gross, pinky, white skin who have to worry about it and I didn't let her get burned, she just played in the surf every day and her skin soaked it up, and anyway this dermatologist was saying that it's out of a knee-jerk political correctness and the sunscreen manufacturers are using this to sell sunscreen to lots of people with darker skin who don't need it and all just because we can't talk about race and skin color frankly—"

"I mean she looks like she's black," the Korean mother said, making a disgusted face, adding, "A Korean mother would not let that happen." Unfortunately Mulan heard the last part of our conversation.

"Why did that mom say that about my tan?" Mulan asked when we got into the car.

I said, "I think it was because she felt I wasn't protecting you enough because I am not Asian."

"Why?" Mulan asked.

"Well, because—well, I'm not sure this mother meant this, but traditionally people don't want their kids' skin, especially their daughters' skin, to be too dark because it would indicate that they worked out in the sun. Historically, darker skin would indicate a lower class of people."

"Why is working out in the sun bad? Roberto works out at the beach. Tom runs on the beach," Mulan said. I realized that for her "working out" meant exercising. Oh my God, we were so bourgeois.

"Not working out in the sun. Working, *out* in the sun. It was considered low status, because that was where the lower-paying jobs were. Are. Were." Argh. I was floundering again.

"Huh?" Mulan said. I was getting too complicated. I had to remember she was in second grade.

"Okay, let me try to explain—"

"Mom, I want to tell you about art class at school; we're making posters and. . . ."

She didn't want to talk about it. And I don't think it was because she was too sensitive or worried about it; I think it was just a boring topic.

Here's what surprised me. After these incidents and discussions, Mulan seemed to forget all about it. She went right back to describing friends who were black without referring to their race. This is another shocking thing about watching a child grow up. Unlike in movies or literature there aren't many moments of irrevocable change in a child based on a new piece of information. Even though I've written about Mulan learning about sex like the event was a thunderbolt of revelation, soon afterward she forgot about it and had to relearn what sex was a little bit over and over again until it really sunk in. It's still happening; she's only twelve. And so it has been with this topic of race, too.

For me, I've learned that both sex and race are loaded, subtle, and complicated concepts. Because of my job parenting Mulan, I've looked at our culture differently, watching how much information any young person must take in to get a handle on sexual norms, expectations, indications of attitudes about race, positive or negative, and how much she will need to pick up on nonverbal clues, visual or physical. Just teaching her enough about stereotypes to get some smarts in her is daunting.

I began this chapter by telling you that Mulan's interest in the subject of race was fleeting, and then undone with a child's typical obliviousness and distractions. I think that may be my own way of dealing with awkward, difficult topics, too.

On that note, I say we drift sideways and then up and away from this subject entirely.

CHAPTER NINETEEN

Phone Bill

Last night before I went to bed, at around eleven-thirty, I decided to do one productive thing. I called AT&T to turn off my brother Bill's cell phone, which I'd been paying for. As I was waiting for an operator to help me, I logged onto my account and saw that my phone bill was four hundred dollars. I was in shock and sputtering as I tried to find out how this could be true, just as the operator answered. He had a thick accent and he identified himself as Stephan. When Stephan logged into my account, he told me my bill was so high because I had a ninety-minute call to Japan, which accounted for $320 of the bill. It was true, I'd been talking to my sister Meg, who lives in Japan. I usually made sure I called from our landline, which is much less expensive. But in the discombobulated state I was in after Bill's death, I wasn't thinking about which phone to use. Stephan said I really should sign up for an international calling plan. I let him go on about this, and how much it would cost per month.

"Can I retroactively sign up for an international calling plan?" I asked.

"I'm sorry, but no," Stephan replied.

"Well, just forget about that," I said. "What I'm really calling for is to turn off another cell phone line I pay for." I gave him Bill's cell phone number.

The whole exchange made me feel weepy and on edge.

"I'm sorry, I cannot," Stephan said.

"What do you mean, you cannot?" I asked, my defenses rising.

"I can't. He's on a contract that doesn't expire until February. I can suspend the account, but you'll still have to pay the minimum monthly fee until February. If you cancel now, your fine will be larger than the monthly fee. It would be better to wait it out."

"What," I began, gathering sad indignation, "if he's *dead*?" The word *dead* came out a little louder than I wanted. Then I burst into tears. I told Stephan that my brother had died. There was silence. I looked around for some tissues. I could hear Stephan cough nervously. Then Stephan told me in a small, quiet voice that his brother had just died, too. I stopped in my tracks.

I asked him where he was. He told me he was in Manila, in the Philippines. "What happened?" I asked him.

He told me his brother died in a car accident. He and his brother had both moved to Manila; their mother lived outside the city. She was devastated. I told him that my mother was devastated, too, and then quickly told him about Bill's alcohol addiction. I tried to keep it short.

Suddenly this connection I was feeling to a person in the ether, this random individual with whom I was oddly associated, all because of my brother Bill, felt vaguely familiar. It had happened before.

When Bill was in jail he would often call me. When you get a call from someone in a correctional facility, it's always a collect call (they are not—or were not—allowed any other kind). When you first answer the phone call there is a long prerecorded announcement about how much it's going to cost. And it costs a lot. The correctional institutions load on fees. Then there's a little space, a little void if you will, where the inmate can say his or her name. Then the prerecorded announcement continues with how expensive this call is going to be.

I always accepted Bill's calls. As I said, Bill and I had great conversations when he was in jail. He was sober and he had lots of time to read. He called me so frequently that he would sometimes make a joke in that little space of time for the inmate to say his name. He'd say, "Who else could it be?" Or even sometimes, "If you're in the middle of something, just don't accept; it's okay."

One night I got a call and I half-listened to the prerecording. Then I heard "Pick up, bitch!" I thought it must be Bill, joking around.

I accepted the call and Bill asked, "What are you doing?" I went on to tell him in detail about a movie I'd just watched. Then I began to realize, too slowly, over maybe a whole minute or two, that I was not speaking with Bill. I was speaking with a different guy, one in the California prison system. *He had randomly called my number!* As soon as I realized that, I said to him, "I'm sorry, I was confused. I'm going to hang up now." And I did.

But then my prison inmate started calling me a lot. At night I would get phone calls from him, and in that little space he'd yell, "Say yes!" Or, "I have no one!" I began to look forward to his calls, to see how creative he could get with his small amount of time. He began to sing songs, or yell, "Baby, baby, baby!" Once he yelled, "Please, please, please!" just like James Brown. Finally he made his way to the phrase that would really get my attention. "I've got a good story for you. . . ."

I accepted the call.

To his credit, he instantly admitted that he did not in fact have a good story. But since I was paying for the call, I asked him why he was in jail. "I robbed a store because I wanted drug money. I didn't hurt anyone. [Pause.] That badly." The pause was exactly the right length. He had a sense of humor. I had no clue if he was really telling the truth.

"Oh," I said. "What's it like in there?"

And then he told me—he really, really told me. I began to feel like he was Charles Dickens getting a penny a word, only for him, every second he got me to stay on the phone was its own victory. I could hear it in his voice. He told me how cramped the prison was, how he was in a cell that was made for four, but there were seven guys in it. I tried to remain skeptical; after all, he was a convicted criminal. He told me about how he had a kid, but his kid's mother was married to someone else. He told me he was from Sacramento. He told me he often had days where he didn't get to go outside at all, and the fluorescent lights were making him go crazy.

I commiserated, because I hated fluorescent lights, too. I told him about how when Joe #10 broke up with me, all I remembered were the horrible fluorescent lights. He said he couldn't imagine anyone breaking up with me. I regretted telling him that. Then I laughed. This was seriously crazy! We talked for about thirty minutes.

That's when he really started calling and calling. He would scream, "I beg you!" with even more intensity. He would yell, "I have no one in my life but you!" I began to speak about him to my friends as "my-guy-in-prison-distinct-from-my-brother-in-prison." My brother in prison got alarmed when I told him. "You can't talk to some loser guy in prison!" Bill said, from prison. "Jesus, Jules, what are you doing?"

I will admit that I accepted the call and talked to "my guy in prison" a couple more times. I was curious and felt strangely bonded with him, like he was a lost orphan at sea and he thought I might be his life raft. But finally I'd had enough. I had to break up with him. I accepted one last call and said, "I am only accepting this call to tell you I will absolutely never accept a call again. You can try and try, but I will not accept. I'm sorry. It's been fun, it's been meaningful, I wish you the best, but it's over." He began to cry. It was actually excruciating. Was I so hard up and so attracted to the strange that I had wound up with the perfect storm of complete wrongness? Or was I just a person with an ear for a good random situation?

"Your brother told you to do this," he said. Because, of course, now he knew about my brother in prison.

"That's bullshit!" Bill said when I told him what my other prison friend said. "He's a big liar," Bill added.

"But you *did* tell me to stop talking to him," I said.

"No, I didn't," Bill said,

"Yes, you did!" I argued.

"No, I swear I did not!" Bill said.

"You're such a liar!" I said.

"Jesus, Jules. I'm in prison, what do you expect?" Bill said. And we both laughed.

Eventually my guy in prison stopped calling me. And after a time, I forgot all about him.

But then, while I was talking with Stephan in the Philippines, I realized that Bill was affording me another wild connection with someone I would probably never otherwise have a conversation with. While I was wondering what had ever happened with "my guy in prison," Stephan pulled me out of my reverie and said, "I'm taking that phone call off your bill."

"What?" I asked.

"Yes," he said, "I can do that. I have the power to do that and I'm doing it, right . . . [I heard many clicks on a computer keyboard] now." I was online looking at my bill, and in a moment, presto, my bill was eighty dollars.

I thanked Stephan profusely. Suddenly I felt suspended with Stephan in space, hovering over the globe, somewhere over the North Pacific. Out of time. I had the same feeling about the guy in prison. I didn't want the moment to end. I realized that when I hung up with the AT&T guy, I would be another stop further away from Bill. In a split second a heavy silence engulfed us. "Thank you so much," I said.

"No problem," Stephan said.

We hung up. It was now after midnight. As I got in bed, I was thinking that things had improved. The last random guy that my brother Bill caused me to get to know had cost me money, but this guy had just saved me $320. And then I thought about Stephan and his sad mother, halfway across the world. I thought about my mother, and all the sad mothers who've just lost sons. Who knows how many and how much grief. An ocean. The North Pacific.

I tried to go to sleep, but accepted that I would probably be looking at the bedroom ceiling for much of the night. In a week my own family would be back at home. And yet, I felt it was me who'd left town.

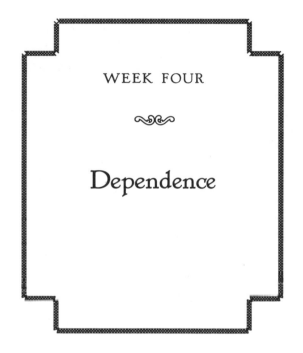

WEEK FOUR

❧

Dependence

CHAPTER TWENTY

My Nemesis

Our home is right across the street from the post office and the library. This location was one of the big reasons I wanted to buy this house. It was like I had these twin little ladies—squat, middle-aged, spare, and sturdy, my post office and my library—there to greet me each morning when I went out to get the paper. "Here we are again!" they say in unison.

The library: "We'll always be here for you."

The post office: "Civilization."

Library: "We may be plain but we are two of the best things about civilization."

Post office: "The mail."

Library: "The books!"

I went to the post office this morning because it was my last chance to send something to Mulan and get it to her before she leaves camp. I'm sending her a tank top from her own closet. I never know what to send her at camp. The first two years she went I sent her junk (Origami paper! Pillowcases that can be signed with Sharpies by her cabin mates!) and this stuff would just eventually come home with her from camp only to be thrown out a few months later. Then I came up with this great idea that I would send her things that I know she already likes, random things I feel she could be wanting, her own stuff. Genius.

Today the weather is turbulent. There's thunder and there's lightning. The heat broke, finally, and with it came a tempest. It was actually storming last night when I was on the phone with the AT&T guy, but I didn't describe that then because I thought it would be too over-the-top. Now that it's still stormy out, I'll tell you. My bedroom flashed light and dark all night from the lightning. Arden cried from under the bed in the Grandma Room downstairs. My cat Val curled up under the sheets. I stared at the ceiling.

The early morning was calm, but now the sky is stirred up again.

I didn't want to stand in line at the post office. I just wanted to get this package off quickly, so I went to the self-mailing machine. There is only one, and there was already a woman using it. I realized it was my Nemesis.

She doesn't know that she is my Nemesis, but she had assumed this position over two years ago.

As I wrote earlier, I walk Arden to the beach nearly every day. Being at the beach for a moment is a great reward for me. I look forward to seeing what the lake is going to look like because, while it's often a surprise—the color, the kind of waves—it always gives me a big wash of calm.

One morning we got to the beach and there was another woman there, with her dog, who was not on a leash. This was a problem, because Arden is aggressive with other dogs. It's the law—wait, "law" sounds too harsh; let's say, the "rule"—the rule is that you have to have your dog on a leash in the park and on the beach. The woman's dog ran up to Arden. When this happens I have no choice but to take him off his leash, because he will be less aggressive with another dog if he's not restrained. I have learned this the hard way, because Arden once bit another dog.

Off leash, dogs usually work out their dominance hierarchies pretty quickly. On leash, dogs know they are restrained. (Michael says that if Arden were a person he would be a policeman: Arden is always barking at other dogs as if to say, "No running!")

The woman with the off-leash dog came up to me.

"Hi!" she said.

"Hi!" I said.

"I think you're supposed to have your dog on a leash," I said, trying to be casual about it.

"They'll work it out," she said.

"I know they will," I said, smiling, trying to be light as air. "But my dog's aggressive, and so if your dog's off leash, it means I *have* to take my dog off his leash or he will bite your dog. Because he'll feel restrained." When I said the word *restrained* I could feel the tendons in my neck lifting up.

"Hey, lighten up, lady," the woman said. "It's a beautiful day." She swept her arm to the side to indicate the sun and water.

I flushed red. We stared at each other for a split second.

Then I turned and Arden followed me. At the end of the sandy area and the beginning of the park proper, I put his leash back on and we walked home. While I walked I tried very hard to enjoy the beautiful day, but couldn't. I came back again and again to her outswept hand indicating the beautiful day. It was true, it *was* a beautiful day.

Also, I hated her, I just hated her.

Months went by. Then one day, on my walk home, I saw her. She was driving up to her house and going in. That's how I came to know where she lived.

Another day, I saw her talking to some workmen out front about some gardening. I imagined the gardener was saying, "You can't plant that here." I imagined she responded with "Hey, lighten up, buddy. It's a beautiful day." Sweeping her arm grandly to indicate her entire front yard. (Her hair was in a ponytail, her type of blond: honey.)

One day as I was walking home, a few months later, I noticed a political placard in my Nemesis's front yard. It was for the Republican congressional candidate from our district. I thought, I knew it. I immediately went home, and made some calls, and offered to volunteer for the Democratic candidate. I gave him money. I befriended him. I worked for two days in a little cramped office, making calls for the Democratic candidate. However, he lost the election.

My Nemesis kept her placard up for a week after the election. Just to stick it to me, I thought.

One day I went to yoga class, and there were a lot of people. Mats were very close together. In plank pose I looked to my left, and there was my Nemesis, our elbows not a foot away from each other. I broke into a sweat; my heart raced. When we did side angle pose I thought I might topple into her. We turned and did a forward bend and my head was practically up her ass. Something must be done! I thought. But what? There was nothing that could be done.

Then one day I was walking back from the beach down her street. I was on the other side of the street from her house. She was standing outside. Then I noticed that her dog was on our side of the street, and, obviously, not on a leash. As I got about ten feet from her dog, she yelled to me: "Can you do me a favor?"

"What?" I yelled back, my heart racing.

"Could you stand for a couple of moments right where you are? I'm training him and this will make a good test."

"Ah . . . okay," I said. Arden was straining on his leash, and barking, and you could tell her dog really wanted to respond. He would glance at Arden, and then look at his master across the street. He was holding himself together impressively, and it was a remarkable display of restraint by both the owner and dog. After a few seconds, my Nemesis gave a little nod with her head, and the dog ran across the street. She really did have a lot of control over her dog. In the meantime, Arden was straining at his leash, trying to run after a squirrel, which caused him to almost run into a bicyclist in the street.

As I walked home, I considered whether I should run for Congress from my home district as a Democrat. Why not? Al Franken is a senator; why couldn't I be in Congress? I wondered if anything short of becoming a congressperson would quell the desire for revenge that I now harbored for my Nemesis.

Two weeks later, new districts were drawn and our home was suddenly in another congressional district, and represented by a Democrat whom I really liked. Curses! Foiled again!

I kept Michael and Mulan up on my travails with my Nemesis. Sometimes when I'd walk in the door with Arden, Mulan would ask, "Did you see your Nemesis today?" My Nemesis actually became instructional, because we looked up the word *nemesis* in the dictionary and discussed its mythological roots.

And now here she was, right in front of me! While I waited behind her as she prepared her parcel, I wondered if I should write on the outside of the package I was sending to Mulan, "My Nemesis is standing right in front of me at the post office!" As I looked around for a pen, my Nemesis turned toward me.

"I think I know you," she said.

"I think you do," I said pointedly. I figured our moment of confrontation had arrived. I looked around; the area with the postal machine was empty. This was good, I thought, in case things got ugly.

"You look very familiar," she said, her eyes narrowing. Suddenly I was struck by the possibility that she might recognize me from television! This would be terrible. I am a little bit famous in the worst way, in that I am vaguely familiar to people. They don't know if they've seen me on television or if I am in their cousin's ride share or if I'm the lunch lady at school. (Actually in the coming year, I *am* going to be the lunch lady at school on Fridays, so now my vague familiarity may cause true confusion.)

"Do you have a kid on the swim team?" she asked.

"I do not," I replied. I accentuated the "t" sound at the end of the word *not*. I was John Wayne.

"Oh, I thought you looked familiar."

"Huh," I said, trying to sound tough. My chin inched upward, as in "What about it, lady?" I tried to make my smile slightly creepy, edging on scary. There was a crack of thunder outside. Perfect timing. I wanted to put fear into her heart.

But my Nemesis did not respond the way I wished. She smiled, shrugged, and then left.

Argh! She defeats me at every turn!

I looked down at my package to Mulan. I didn't write, "My Nemesis was standing in front of me as I mailed this," on it because I became aware that I was behaving toward this woman in "an extreme" manner instead of "a reasonable" manner—a distinction that I often bring up with Mulan.

Unexpectedly, the fact of Mulan's absence from our house tore into my chest like a knife. I missed her terribly. I could hardly stand it. I wanted to walk in the house and tell her about my encounter with my Nemesis and we would surely laugh together. Mulan would probably tease me and I would pretend to be annoyed. This would allow me to tease her about something she was obsessing about. I missed our daily interaction. How should she wear her hair? I even miss nudging her to get her piano practice finished for the day. My exasperation at her inability to simply close her dresser drawers after getting something out of them, and pick up her friggin' underwear off the floor, seems quaint and sweet.

How did she go away for a month? What kind of parent

would allow such a thing? How will I stand it when she goes to college? What arrogance did I have, feeling so superior, thinking how I needed to be *alone,* as if I didn't need anyone. Even implying that everyone needed me so much! That is such bullshit. I have to take that out of this book. I'm so bored with myself I could scream.

And what about Michael? Where is my husband? I'm tired of eating alone, and where is his familiar focused hunch over *The New York Times* every morning? His glasses up on his forehead as he peers into the face of his iPhone reading me the best tweets of the day? I long for him to come through the back door with his basket of vegetables from the garden, even though I am usually irritated by this because it means having to figure out what the hell to do with all those vegetables, vegetables that he refuses to put in the refrigerator because he feels it ruins their freshness! Which in reality means that many of them will start rotting on the kitchen counter. I even miss the whir of his apnea machine at night. He is my handsome masked man, sleeping next to me in bed. Where is he?

I long for the fall, when school starts and everything is routine. How am I going to get through this last week? This whole idea that I was going to figure out something important about myself during this time is so pretentious! There's nothing wrong. I'm just irritated and annoyed like everybody is. There's no big secret revelation. I just needed a little break.

After I mailed my package I went home and the house seemed empty and dark. It felt like a stage, set for a show about a family home, only it was not a shooting day. Everything seemed especially inert and lifeless.

CHAPTER TWENTY-ONE

A Proposal at Starbucks

Last spring, Mulan was giving me advice about how I should behave when I came to the school and looked at the science fair projects. Mulan did not want me to talk to any of the other kids—and she especially did not want me to tell any student that I was her mother. She was worried I would ask too many questions or stick out among the throng. The bottom line is that she was embarrassed by me. She thought that at the fifth-grade science fair I had laughed too loudly and made too many sounds of joy that were too audible when I encountered projects I liked.

Okay, fine. I accept that. I was embarrassed by my own mother, too, starting around this age. I wanted to remind Mulan that she hadn't always felt this way about me. In fact, there was a time when she even wanted us to get married.

When Mulan and I first met Michael it was very exciting—we had this new person in our lives. I had read some advice about how to help a kid deal with a mother's dating. The advice was that you shouldn't even introduce the new man (or woman) to the children until you've been dating for six to nine months! But our situation didn't allow for that. (Frankly I can't imagine a situation that would.) Michael, Mulan, and I met each other at the same moment. After the initial visit, Michael stayed with us when he came to town. This was common for Mulan and me, anyway. We had a lot of guests. In particular, my two closest friends; Jim (who came with me to China) and Gino (who lives in Milwaukee but who often works in Los Angeles) were regular houseguests. They were like family. The only difference was that Michael stayed in my bedroom. Mulan barely seemed to register that as different from Jim and Gino.

Then she had this terrible realization, and I could see it cross her face. Michael wasn't going. He was staying. He was giving attention to her, but he was taking attention away from her mother. This was not a good development.

I realize now, in retrospect, that Mulan thought *she and I* were a couple. Here's an example. Friends of ours, a couple, invited Mulan and me over for an early dinner with some other couples. She was around age five or six at this time. I think they invited Mulan because they'd just adopted a baby themselves, who was only a few weeks old. When we got there, their big long dining room table was set. Ten place settings along a long wooden table, five couples. All of them married or partners. But my partner was Mulan. She was the only child besides the infant, who was sleeping off to the side of the dining room table in a bassinette.

Toward the end of the meal, around eight o'clock, Mulan yawned with her arms outstretched, in a confident, languorous manner, leaning back in her chair. Her arm landed on my far shoulder, familiarly, proprietary. Like a spouse's would. Then, with startling confidence, she leaned in to the table, her arm still around my shoulders, and said to the group, "I think we should get going. I have to get up early tomorrow." She turned toward me and said, "And I think you do, too, right?"

Everyone at the table laughed. Mulan asked me on the way home, "Why was everyone laughing?" "Oh," I said, "it's just, you're getting to be so grown-up." But really— to Mulan we *were a couple.*

After Michael made us into a threesome, and this idea registered in her head, she rebelled. A few times when Michael and I were holding hands, she would come up and pull them apart, and forcefully put her hand in mine. Once she put her little face a few inches from Michael's and said somberly, with a Clint Eastwood–like simmer, "Get. Out. Of. Our. Lives."

She began to have major fits, melting down more often than usual. She became defiant. I could not bend her will, or cleverly work around her when her behavior became obstinate. To make matters worse, Michael began to think of Mulan as an unruly and difficult child. I was at a loss in dealing with her tantrums at first. This was a new behavior and I hadn't developed a strategy for it yet. Telling Michael this seemed like a lame excuse. "She's perfect when you're not around!" Right.

I lurched around, trying out new ways to deal with the outbursts. Simultaneously, Michael and I were really falling in love. It was incredibly difficult to hide it, although I did try as best I could. Mulan began to break into my bedroom more and more often. Suddenly she wanted to sleep with me all the time. We would all have a good evening together, and Mulan would get into her pajamas and into my bed, announcing, "This is where I sleep now." I think Michael was thinking, Is this normal or do they have some deeply disturbing relationship? I was actually wondering the same thing.

Looking back, I am amazed I lived through this time. It was traumatic.

One day, Mulan and I were sitting in Starbucks, me with my coffee and her with her hot chocolate. "Why don't we get married?" she asked me.

"Oh, honey," I said, floundering, "two women can't get married." (That was lame, I know, but I was scrambling.)

"Yes they can," Mulan replied.

"Oh right. Yes they can," I stammered, "But Mulan, I am your *mother*."

"So?" Mulan asked.

"Well, mothers and daughters can't get married."

"Why not?" Mulan asked.

"Well, because they're already mother and daughter."

"But why can't we be mother and daughter and married, too?"

"Because we're so different in age," I said. Again this was lame.

"Why does that matter?" Mulan asked. I continued to fumble.

"All our references will not be the same—our music, politics—it's too big an age range."

"And why does that matter?"

I regained my equilibrium. I began to think a little straighter. "Well, because the feeling of love that two people have for each other who are married is a different feeling than mothers and fathers and their children have." Suddenly, images of Woody Allen and Soon-Yi Previn burst into my mind. I almost said, "I'm not into young girls." But I thought that Mulan would probably take that the wrong way. She'd think, Why did you adopt a daughter if you aren't "into young girls"?

My adult brain (or what passes for an adult brain) finally kicked in. I said, "It's a distinctly different feeling they have for each other that you will not understand until you get older and go through puberty and feel a sexual attraction for another person. It's love, but a different kind of love. Someday you will understand, but that's the best explanation I can give you right now. We just cannot get married."

"Oh," Mulan said, slumping in her chair.

Now I have an almost thirteen-year-old child, who is not having tantrums anymore. She will, however, challenge the truth of this very chapter. It will become further evidence in her arsenal pointing to why I should never talk when anyone else is around. But to be honest, it's much easier to be a weirdo in your child's eyes than trapped in the psychodrama that shrouds the beginning of a major new relationship.

Looking back, I think I met Michael at just the right moment. Mulan was in kindergarten. I think if it had been even one year later it would have been twice as difficult. I have several friends who are single mothers and after their children were in first or second grade, they avoided any new romantic relationship. They figured it would just be easier to wait until their children were gone, after high school. I think I probably would have been like that. Although it's easy to say that from here.

CHAPTER TWENTY-TWO

An Education

Mulan's first preschool was a very fancy, upscale type of place. The tuition was about the same that my nephew, Nick (Bill's son), is currently paying for his university education. The mothers were so young and beautiful (and thin, God, so thin!) it was discombobulating. The ratio of teachers to students was like 1 to 3. The place was opulent. I said to my friend Jeff, who has three kids who all went through this fancy preschool, "Why are there so many incredibly beautiful women here? It's like a beauty pageant."

He said, "A lot of women come to Hollywood because they are very beautiful. They come from all over America, in fact, all over the world. They come here because this is where you can really exploit your luck at being born gorgeous. Maybe they want to be actresses. Maybe the part of being an actress they like most is the part where people admire your beauty. Sometimes they make it in show business. Most, however, do not. Then, you have a lot of very successful men here in Hollywood. Many of them were overlooked in high school. They have a deep psychological need to be with a knockout. This need is a gasoline that powers their desire to dominate. The women decide that their best bet is to marry these men and seal the deal by having a couple of kids. They're like anyone assessing their prospects in the face of their declining value because they're getting older. Can you blame them? It's a smart move. They came to be actresses, but end up being full-time mothers. And many of them do not work outside the home, and they have the time, and the desire, to hang out at the school, parading their beauty for all of us to enjoy."

Wow. I could see that was true. One day I was on the playground and saw a mother who had given birth two months previous. She was holding her baby, and she was wearing a very thin, undersized, fashionably ripped tank top that exposed her already flat belly. I looked to my left and saw a strikingly good-looking woman and I thought, Jesus Christ, these mothers are absurdly beautiful, I mean, that mother looks like Catherine Zeta-Jones.

The woman came closer. It was Catherine Zeta-Jones.

I did find friends at the preschool. A group of parents in Mulan's class and I all bonded deeply. We lived relatively close to each other. We mingled at birthday parties, we came to be each other's best friends. But it was still otherworldly. No one was a single parent like me.

"Where are all the single parents?" I asked my friend Jeff. "I thought the world was filled with single parents like me. Aren't I just the kind of mother that Dan Quayle was all up in arms about? Where are they?"

"Wait till second grade; a lot of divorces will happen around then. Then there'll be other single mothers."

"Why second grade?" I asked him.

"Because kids are hard and parents . . . well, a lot of parents turn on each other. It's like they didn't realize that by having kids they were signing up for that *Dirty Jobs* reality show. Little kids put a lot of pressure on parents; a lot of people realize that the person they joined with for "America's Toughest Jobs" was a model who liked to be pampered, or an actor who is completely self-absorbed, or a film executive who feels little need to do anything with the family. And now they are at sea and the boat is rocking. A hate grows. Resentment takes root. Weirdly, they often wait until the kid is about six or so before really calling it quits. And that's when it all gets a lot better! You'll see, a lot of divorces around first and second grade."

I shrugged and hoped I never had such a cynical view of marriage.

In the meantime, I began to really dislike the elite environment of the fancy school. I wanted my kid in a school with a real-world feel. Other parents at the preschool, in our little group of friends, felt the same. We decided to send our kids to our local public school. We all agreed we would get involved and try to make the public school as good a place as possible.

As soon as Mulan was at the public school I felt much better. The parents all looked exhausted and haggard and beaten down by the reality of life. Nobody was trying to hang out at the school, smiling, with their Intelligentsia coffee cups. I was so happy.

When I went into the front office of the public school and donated two hundred dollars for office supplies, the principal's assistant nearly burst into tears. At the fancy school, the annual benefit cost $350 per ticket just to attend, and then the raffles and auctions were on top of that. I did a benefit performance for our new public school. I performed a monologue I had recently written. The school decided to charge *ten dollars a ticket*. And they had forms for people who might want to come and couldn't afford the ten dollars, in which case their ticket fee would be waived. When I raised four hundred dollars from this performance, I had to stop the school from putting a huge banner outside the school congratulating me for my efforts. How could this school and the fancy preschool be less than one mile from each other?

The whole experience made me feel bad about *ever* having had my kid at the fancy preschool. I hated the class system, which in California was not so much about race as it was about money.

And like Jeff said, around first and second grade, parents began to get divorced. Women began to slide up to me and say, "I'm a single mother, too."

But this began to bother me. They weren't single parents. They were divorced parents. Many of them got child support. They got weekends free because their child was with their ex.

"I would kill for an ex!" I said to my friend Jeff.

"Having an ex is not always as dreamy as it sounds," Jeff said.

Then I began to notice that this public school really wasn't as fantastic as I thought. Budgets were being cut. Teacher assistants were losing their jobs. Classes had thirty kids. I began to see the exhausted looks on parents' faces differently. They looked more like they were beginning to see that the system was rigged against them. They couldn't afford the fancy schools. They looked like they were trying to just make it through the week.

During one spring, I was helping with the student fair, making cotton candy with another mother. The mother and I surveyed the playground. To me it looked idyllic, kids of all races and ethnicities, food from around the world, as we listened to beautiful Caribbean music, which alternated with American blues, and then traditional Korean music. The sun was shining.

Then the mother said casually, "You know, these public schools are really best for two types of kids. One type is the kid who needs extra help and attention. Kids who have a real mental disability. Or the opposite type. If your kid is very, very smart they can get into the accelerated, well-funded high-honor school. But if your kid is middle-of-the-road, it's actually not a great place." This particular mother had a son with autism, and after she told me that, I began to notice how well the public school system was serving her and her son. For example, there was a person assigned to hang out with her son individually, in each class. This companion would help her son integrate into the school system as best as he could. This was all paid for with public funds. (Which I think is great; I'm just sayin'.)

Then one of Mulan's friends tested into the genius kid program, which got her out of our public school and into one of those elite public schools that that mother was talking about. When we visited her friend, the school was on a campus with expansive green manicured lawns, and white, freshly painted buildings with Greek columns, overlooking the Pacific Ocean. They provided a bus to pick up kids and transport them, an hour each way, to and from school, all paid for with public funds. Wow.

I began to look into what it would take to get Mulan into this school or one like it. It turns out there is a fairly complicated point system that you have to participate in from the beginning. You earn "points" for test scores, but also for having applied to these schools in the past and *not* being chosen. Being rejected actually conferred benefits. Mulan could get extra points for being Asian, but I couldn't go back in time and collect all the points needed for testing as far back as kindergarten. I realized I had blown it. Part of the reason was that I looked at the testing itself with disdain. I didn't like how some parents were working the system. I didn't think their kids were necessarily so spectacular; they just had a parent who was an active, nearly full-time advocate figuring the system out. But although my inaction and my disdain had left me with my principles intact, I was not in a position to get Mulan into the best public school I could.

Then Mulan started second grade. When I went to the parent orientation with Michael, we noticed that the teacher looked a little checked out. School had been in session for only two days. She was older and wore a printed dress that looked like it was made out of feed-sack cloth. She had really big bags under her eyes and her voice sounded scratchy and hoarse. She did not smile. The first thing she said was "I've been in the system for thirty-two years." *The system.* Michael leaned over to me and said, ". . . and nobody can kick me out now."

Afterward I said to Michael, "That teacher looks like she's about to have a nervous breakdown."

"She doesn't seem so bad," Michael said. "Maybe she's just realistic."

But I turned out to be right. Mulan's second-grade teacher did go on "bed rest" after only four weeks of school. Two weeks later she took early retirement and for the rest of the year Mulan had a new substitute almost every week.

Mulan never liked any of them. All of them called her "Tara" because that was her legal first name and she had to tell them she was "Mulan." She hated this because it reminded her how much her teacher didn't know her. She never got her homework returned. Finally she had a teacher she liked a lot. He really stood out because he was her substitute for two weeks. And he called her Mulan, not Tara.

"Maybe he'll take a permanent position as second-grade teacher!" I said to Mulan hopefully.

The next week Mulan told me he was gone. "Oh no," I said.

"He got a recurring on *Bones*," Mulan said, sighing. *Bones* was a TV show on at the time. My God, Mulan knew the definition of *recurring*. (It means you are on a TV show intermittently but regularly.)

I'd had enough of this school. Michael and I were getting married and the plan was that he was going to live with us in L.A. and somehow commute to do his business work. Spring came around and we did get married.

However, during the summer between Mulan's second and third grade, she went to camp (the one she's at right now) for the first time, for two weeks. At only eight years old, she was really nervous about going to camp, even though she had campaigned to go in the first place. Michael and I planned to spend the time she was gone camping ourselves, in a tent, all around California. This meant that we couldn't get regular mail (the only mail the camp allowed). I told Mulan to send any mail for me to my mother, in Spokane. That way my mother could read me what Mulan wrote over the phone.

"I don't know if I want to read this to you," my mother said about the first postcard she got from Mulan addressed to me.

"Just read it," I said.

"Okay . . . she wrote, 'Dear Mom, I don't miss you. Love, Mulan.' "

I laughed really hard. But the thing was, I knew what Mulan meant. Before Mulan went to camp she had gotten really worried about missing me too much. We talked about it a lot. What would she do? She even said, "What if I can't stop crying because I miss you so much? What then?" We talked about ways to cope. She had a special picture of me that she could put under her pillow, along with a small flashlight. This way she could look at the picture in the middle of the night if she needed to.

So I was actually relieved that Mulan wrote me that. She was telling me she was okay.

That night, by our campfire in the Sierra Nevada, I thought about Mulan's postcard. I realized that if Mulan was resilient enough to go to camp where she didn't know a soul, and make friends quickly and figure out how to be happy, she could change schools and it would be okay. I asked Michael if he would consider Mulan and I moving to the Chicago area instead of his moving to Los Angeles. He agreed. Even though he had moved around a lot as a kid growing up, and went to many different schools, and he really didn't like that, he said he could see that Mulan would be better off getting out of Los Angeles at that moment. This meant Michael would have to give up his dream of living in California.

"The schools are great in Wilmette," he said quietly, looking into the campfire. Wilmette, huh. It was all I could do not to jump up and rush to a place where I could get cell reception so I could start googling schools in Wilmette.

When I finally did, it appeared the schools were fantastic. The high school, New Trier, was consistently written up as one of the best public schools in the country. That was it. We were moving.

We moved during Mulan's third-grade winter break. We bought our minivan, and planned our Odyssey with the whole gang. We had a moving company come and take our belongings. Norma, Michael's mother, decided to sell her house in Washington, D.C., and rent my house from us. This way we could keep the house, and Michael and I plan to move back in as soon as Mulan goes to college.

So we loaded up the minivan. Val was going to stay in the front part of the van, and Arden was to be relegated to the back end. When the house was empty and we were all in the vehicle, Arden snuck out of the car and ran back in the house, traumatized by its emptiness and the unfamiliarity of what seemed to be happening. He didn't want to go. We had to drag him on his leash back to the car as he whimpered. We headed out: Mulan, me, Arden, and Val all looking back at our house as Michael drove us away.

We drove through warm, sunny (not very humid) weather into snow and cold. When we drove into the driveway of our new house, on Christmas Eve, the car temperature reading for the outside was fifteen below zero. But I was as excited as I'd ever been about anything.

We slept on sleeping bags upstairs because our furniture hadn't arrived yet from Los Angeles. On December 26, we took the Metra train to downtown Chicago and went to the federal building. We went before a family court judge who completed the adoption proceedings so that Michael was now Mulan's legal father. Mulan wanted to change her name from Tara Mulan Sweeney to Mulan Sweeney Blum. The judge sat on a traditional bench, which was high above the three of us. She leaned over and asked Mulan, "Is he going to be a good dad?"

"I think so. It seems like it," Mulan answered.

"Who's funnier, your mother or your father?" the judge asked.

"Oh, my father is much funnier," Mulan replied.

I laughed.

"But has he gotten *paid* to be funny?" the judge asked.

"Oh, no. No, he hasn't. Not yet, anyway," Mulan answered.

Mulan's grade school was so close I could hear the school bell ring. The teachers at her new school were enthusiastic and dedicated to the point of parody. I was living the dream.

When I stood outside the elementary school on Mulan's first day, waiting for her to emerge, I waited with a lot of other caretakers. They all looked like college students to me, and that seemed right because we are so close to Northwestern University. I could imagine that a lot of students would be available to be babysitters after school.

But no. They were not college students. They were the *other mothers*.

They all looked so young. I looked so old.

Three times, and I want to repeat that, three times, people said to Mulan, "Mulan, your grandmother is here." Referring to me. As her grandmother.

It was true that I had let my hair go gray. But I thought I had that youthful, athletic, Seattle-y look of a woman who does not want chemicals on her hair. So natural! But my gray hair didn't give me that look. I found I really just looked like I was someone's grandmother.

Also, I am really old.

I decided to start dying my hair brown.

So far the schools here have exceeded their promise. Mulan began to thrive immediately. She has a lot of friends; they all live within walking distance. They sometimes meet up at the library across the street. They ride their bikes to the beach and run into each other on corners and spontaneously hang out.

We pay nearly three times the taxes here that I pay on my house in Los Angeles. (My small bungalow in Los Angeles is worth exactly the same as our four-bedroom house here.) But it's public school. That means a lot to me. I went to Catholic schools, and while I have a lot of fond memories of my education, I didn't want that for Mulan. If it were up to me, there wouldn't be any private schools. And schools wouldn't have their budgets tied to property taxes, either. Every kid should be in a school as good as Mulan's school is now.

On Memorial Day Michael and I watched a parade, which made its way right in front of our house. We sat on the parking strip and watched Boy Scouts with flags and fire trucks go by, along with parents with toddlers in red wagons and dogs on leashes.

"We live in the quintessential small town," I said to Michael.

"No, we live in a town, where if you have enough money, you can buy the small-town experience," Michael said, smiling.

I have lived a particularly privileged life. I was able to choose not to be a mother, and I was able to choose to be a mother, on my own terms. I was able to choose to move to a place with good public schools, just because we can afford to pay these kinds of taxes. I was enabled by a system where the deck was stacked in my favor, and now I am able to stack it in my daughter's favor. I am well aware that I am lucky beyond reckoning.

So Michael is right. We have bought our way into this "small-town" experience. But I'll take it. I love it. Right now, for us, it's perfect.

CHAPTER TWENTY-THREE

Hinky Dink Is Sinking

I felt an overwhelming urge to go to the Calvary Catholic Cemetery, which is about four miles from my house. This is the one with our family crypt where all those great-aunties are buried. I had to tell them about Bill. Like they wouldn't know if I didn't go there. Of course, I know this is not literally true, but I had to indulge that part of me that still believes this, like a child who must be satisfied.

I've taken Arden for walks in this cemetery. Last year, I was looking for a particular headstone, of Michael "Hinky Dink" Kenna. I was surprised when I realized that the headstones are sinking underneath the grass. I didn't know. I didn't know until

Arden scratched at something hard and concrete underneath the lawn.

You see, there are swathes of the cemetery that appear to be grassy parkland. They seem to be empty, waiting for you and me and anyone else who might enjoy a nice burial plot. But no. It's not empty. It's filled with bodies. Headstones are just an inch or two underneath the turf. Sometimes a name peeks out—part of a last name, a "Mc" or an "O," and that's it. So many Marys. And variations of Mary—Marion, Marie, Meg, and on and on. The dead are disappearing.

It turns out cemetery upkeep is all about lawn care. Cutting the grass around headstones is tedious and labor intensive. The Catholic Church is busy scrambling to pay off former (understandably disgruntled) altar boys who were molested and everyone else who's just woken up and wondered, What the hell *was* that Bible passage about, anyway? Don't get me wrong. I have a rather intense, affectionate, love-hate relationship with the Catholic Church. You might have guessed that by now.

The point is, the church isn't allocating the money needed for the upkeep of the headstones. The lawn mowers ride right over them, and now they're dropping down. I imagine the Dead gasping for air, as if their sinking headstones were their mouths. The grass is greedy; it wants that space.

But still, I wanted to find Hinky Dink. Let me explain.

My grandmother Henrietta was the eldest of seven girls, all born in Chicago between 1894 and 1905. Her father, Michael Ryan, died in 1906 when Henrietta was twelve years old. Of her seven sisters, only two married—Henrietta and her sister Marion. The other sisters became lifelong, dedicated (and unmarried) public school teachers. After Henrietta's father died, her mother became known as Papa Ryan. Pictures of her reveal a sturdy and stout, Jane Darwellian–type of matron. (Jane Darwell was an actress in many John Ford films; most famously she played Ma Joad in *The Grapes of Wrath*.) The point is that she had that meaty, weary look. (She's starting to show up now and then when I look in the mirror. What is she doing in there?)

One day my grandmother and I were together at her house in Spokane. I was in my twenties by then and already living in Los Angeles. Henrietta opened a book and out floated an obituary from the *Chicago Tribune*, dated November 12, 1938, for John "Bathhouse" Coughlin. The obit described his life as a politician, and also described his political partner Michael "Hinky Dink" Kenna, who was an alderman of the First Ward. Henrietta told me that Hinky Dink took care of their family financially after her father died. She described Hinky Dink as a cousin. Or she might have said "like" a cousin. I saved the obituary and I have appreciated particular phrases. For example, "Coughlin rose, like a florid Phoenix, from the ashes of the great Chicago fire." A phoenix! And when describing his political partnership with Hinky Dink, it reads, "They were free handed alms givers and made many friends. They formed a Damon and Pythias political team within the Democratic Ranks." Damon and Pythias! You don't read references like that in the paper anymore.

When I asked Henrietta how her father died, she made some remark about how, after having seven girls in a row, his hair turned white and he died. We laughed, yes—how terrible to have seven daughters. But now I regret that I didn't ask, "Ha, ha. No, really. What happened?" Later I learned that Hinky Dink's district contained most of the gambling houses and brothels. In fact, both Hinky Dink and Bathhouse John owned bars. They gave away free drinks to anyone who voted for them. Once alcohol was outlawed, the National Crime Syndicate gained momentum and power, which culminated in Al Capone being in charge. (Oh, you Christian temperance ladies, what were you thinking?) The point is, that was the end of Hinky Dink and Bathhouse John.

I learned that one of Hinky Dink's closest friends was a police captain in charge of the First Ward. His name was Michael Ryan, and he pointedly turned a blind eye to all the unlawful activity flagrantly taking place in his district. His career ended in disgrace. This may or may not have been my great-grandfather—every tenth Irish guy in Chicago seems to have been named Michael Ryan.

My cousin Catherine Twomey (a descendant of Marion, the other sister of my grandmother who married) is the one who has found out all this information about our family and it was she who took me to see this crypt at Calvary Cemetery. The crypt has five of the sisters, as well as their parents: Michael Ryan and Mary Donohue Ryan. And Mary's mother: Mary Collins Ryan. They all came from Limerick, Ireland. There are others buried there, too, for example, Hannah Hanley, who was a cousin (or she might have been "like" a cousin). Hannah lived for 102 years, from 1826 to 1928. Catherine found an article in the *Chicago Tribune* about Hannah on her one hundredth birthday. In the article, Hannah described coming from Ireland, in her forties, and getting a job as a housekeeper in New York City, on the Upper East Side. One day when she was sweeping the front steps she heard people in the streets yelling about something. She was told that the president had been shot—President Abraham Lincoln. Somehow Hannah Hanley ended up living with Papa Ryan, and my grandmother and all her sisters, here in Chicago.

Henrietta used to tell me how the family would go to Calvary Cemetery as an all-day outing. They boarded the trolley downtown and took a picnic lunch. They laid down blankets and ate and lounged alongside their buried relatives. There were others doing the same thing, a common way to spend a day. They got to know the descendants of the deceased in nearby tombs. When I visit our family's crypt, I think about Henrietta standing there, and the other people who were visiting buried loved ones, who are now probably interred alongside them. These people were all religious and ostensibly had faith in an afterlife, and they were deeply connected to the reality of death. Today, while many people do not believe in an afterlife (I am among them), people seem much more disconnected from the fact that they're going to die. (I hope I am not among those.)

When I adopted Mulan I became much less interested in my family's history. In fact, I felt it bordered on unseemly to develop deeper interests in my ancestry, when Mulan won't have that opportunity. My general attitude is that people live and move around, they fall in love and create kids, there are economic and environmental upturns and downturns, people move and shift some more. I see all of us as on a river, floating along, bumping into one another.

A couple of years ago, Mulan was doing a social studies section on immigration. She was asked to write an essay about the recent immigrants in her family. She became really interested in the project. She asked for stories and both Michael and I told her some things. Her interest was poignant and touching.

She didn't include my father's family, by which I mean Henrietta's family, the story I just recounted. I will print her essay here.

IMMIGRATION IN MY FAMILY
by Mulan Sweeney Blum

This is how my family came to America.

My mother's maternal great Grandmother, Katherine Ibach came from Odessa, Russia, at the age of eighteen. She came because her mom died and her father remarried, so Katherine left and went to America. She got a job as a maid in South Dakota. There she met Joseph Schatz who was also from Odessa, Russia. They had eleven children, and they spoke German at home. (Their ninth child was named Marie. She was my mom's grandmother.) They were Catholics who'd moved from Germany to Russia because Russia offered free farmland. But when the revolution in Russia started happening, they wanted to get out of there and come here to America.

My great grandfather, on my mother's side, was named Tom Ivers and he was born in Dublin, Ireland. He almost died at age eight during the Easter Uprising in Dublin because a bullet went right over his head while he stood in line for bread. At age fourteen he got in a fight with his dad and so he snuck out onto a boat that he thought was going to London. But it turned out that the boat was going to South America! They made him work on the boat when they found him. After two years in South America, he took another boat to New York City. He sold newspapers on the streets. He got into construction. He went to Yakima, Washington, to build a dam, and then he met Marie, who was working in a factory canning fruit.

On my dad's maternal side, my great grandfather Marcus Manna left home in Warsaw, Poland, at age twelve because his father thought he should leave the ghetto to make a better living. He had seven brothers. First he went to Basel, Switzerland, where his brother Max worked in a hat factory. He got Marcus a job there. When he was seventeen he went on the S.S. *Lincoln* ship to New York in 1913 and went through Ellis Island.

My dad's grandmother, Fannie Rosnoff, was born in the Ukraine, in Russia. She came to America when she was two years old with her mother and three other siblings. Marcus and Fannie met on a picket line in New York City. They were striking to get better pay. Marcus became a union organizer.

I came from Guangzhou, China. I came because I was adopted. I am the newest person to come to America in my family. I was seventeen months old when I was adopted by my mom, a single woman who lived in Los Angeles. Then she married my dad, Michael, who then adopted me. We moved here because my dad has a business building scientific instruments in Evanston, Illinois.

I laughed when I read about myself: *a single woman who lived in Los Angeles.*

I was so thankful to her teacher and school, because I hadn't thought about how Mulan is an immigrant, and she is from a long line of immigrants, and that this fact connects her to my family as surely as genes do.

I enjoy going to the Calvary Cemetery in Evanston just as much as I enjoy going to Holy Cross Cemetery in Spokane. I like to walk where my relatives walked. I like to look at landmarks and buildings that my ancestors looked at. I like to rub my hands across the wood pews in the churches where my family worshipped, knowing that it was likely that, at some point, they sat right there, too. It causes me to have that numinous feeling that C. S. Lewis wrote about—a sense of awe, and a sense of being suspended out of time.

My family's ancestry is riddled with people showing up out of nowhere. Children who came from Ireland whose birth dates make it impossible for them to be the siblings they claim to be, or just extra people who show up, like Hannah Hanley did, and live with families for years and years. I think this is common of all families.

I recently learned that paternity is misattributed in the human species at a rate of 10 percent. This surprised me. In fact, the 10 percent figure is the low estimate! Just think of it—10 percent of the population believe someone is their biological father who is *not* their biological father. That really sealed the deal for me— these stories I have learned, it doesn't matter if they are of people to whom I am actually related. It doesn't matter if Hinky Dink is a cousin or "like" a cousin. They're all people who influenced people who influenced me. Their stories of triumph and tragedy, struggle and loss, lie in the peat bog of my psyche. Because of this, those influences—like ingredients in a soup—will have an impact, subtle or strong, on Mulan.

There's a sculpture here in Chicago on the South Side, in Washington Park, that perfectly portrays the way I imagine our ancestors. It depicts one hundred people of all ages and types in a state of movement before a still figure who is watching them. It's called *The Fountain of Time,* and it was inspired by Henry Austin Dobson's poem "Paradox of Time," which has these first lines:

Time goes, you say? Ah, no!
Alas, time stays, we go.

When I went on an Architecture Foundation tour of Calvary Cemetery last October, I told our guide, Mary Jo, that I had some kind of connection to Hinky Dink Kenna. She insisted that I stay after her tour. She said we could find his headstone together.

As we searched, Mary Jo pointed out John "Bathhouse" Coughlin's large mausoleum. She told me he died fifty thousand dollars in debt, but he had already built his lavish memorial. We scrounged around in the grass and found Hinky Dink's gravestone, which was small, and like the others nearby, sinking under the grass. We even had to pull back the grass to read his name. Mary Jo told me that when Hinky Dink died in 1946, he had more than a million dollars in the bank. He left instructions that his relatives use $33,000 to create a beautiful memorial grave site. But they didn't. They kept the money and got him an $85 headstone instead.

Okay, so maybe Hinky Dink was not such a wonderful man. Or maybe his relatives were the horrible ones. Who knows? (I think the lesson is that, if you want a big memorial in the cemetery, you should build it before you die.)

My mother and I spoke this morning and she told me that she's going to bury Bill in the same grave with Michael, my other brother who died. I guess you can bury two people in one plot at that cemetery. They will be near my father's grave. He died in 2004. My mother already has her plot next to his. My mother said, "Julia, you should get a plot. This is your chance to get into some real estate in Spokane."

When I was young, my father used to listen to a record of Brendan Behan reading autobiographical stories. Brendan Behan was an Irish storyteller, playwright, and activist. My father said Behan had died of "the Irish disease" and I swear to you that for many years I thought he meant storytelling, not alcohol. I think my urge to perform, and specifically to perform true stories from my own life, is my way of coping. Just like alcohol is for some people.

But the storytelling urge is not particular to the Irish. It's in everyone. In fact it's how our brains, every single one of our brains—not particular to any ethnicity—makes sense of the world. We tell ourselves how it all went, how this happened and how that happened and how it could happen in the future. Just like I've been doing intensely for this entire month.

I wanted to be alone, but I am actually always alone. I can work harder to keep the quiet flame of solitude burning inside me, so I don't get too burned-out doing things for others. I like to do a lot for people, and then be adored for my efforts. I get annoyed when I'm not appreciated enough. I want an audience, even at home. Also, I think I'm in some deep competition with my mother. Showing her, or maybe God—that fellow I dismissed so many years ago—how competent I am. How well I can run/decorate/manage a house and family. I think my mother was in some kind of competition with her own mother, too.

Maybe all women do this to some degree. I guess in the end, if it's not one thing, it really *is* your mother!

In the end I'll probably be buried in a plot at Holy Cross Cemetery. Life is both short and incredibly long. Who cares if the table is set properly or the cat vomit is wiped up? Okay, stepping in the cat vomit would be really gross. It seriously needs to get wiped up, people.

But, as my Nemesis reminded me so pointedly, "Hey, lighten up, lady. It's a beautiful day." Recasting her as Papa Ryan makes her quip less toxic.

In fact, loving and wise.

CHAPTER TWENTY-FOUR

Tomorrow They Arrive

The heat wave has abated. It's only going to be 87 degrees today. The weather this summer was frankly a bit frightening. I'm not sure what's in store for our future climate. From what I've read, the future is so bright we'll have to wear shades (but not exactly for the reasons that Timbuk3 wrote those lyrics).

This last spring I came home one day from the lake and said to Michael, "The water was the most amazing blue, a blue I thought was possible only in the Caribbean. And clear, too, so clean and clear, I could see right through it. I was so moved by its beauty."

Michael said, "Oh, that's because the zebra mussels, originally from Russia, have infested the lake and eaten all the algae. It's causing mass death and destruction for the indigenous water animals in the lake, but, yes, a by-product of this catastrophe is that the lake is a brighter, lighter, clearer blue."

"Oh," I said, my beatific smile turning into a grimace. It reminded me of when I first moved to Los Angeles and found the sun setting to be especially magical, the sky turning such a deep orange. Then I learned that the thick pollution was dramatically enhancing those gorgeous sunsets.

Tomorrow I'm driving to the airport and picking up Mulan and Michael, who are arriving at nearly the same time, in the early afternoon. They are coming from opposite directions, Michael from Switzerland and Mulan from California. For me this seems to enhance the impact of their arrival. My anticipation is high, and I can't wait to get my hands on both of them.

In the next month we'll go on our family vacation, to the San Juan Islands off the coast of Seattle, and then on to Bill's funeral in Spokane. This month seemed to do its trick. I already don't want to repeat this long month's journey into night again next summer. I'm sated. The itch has been scratched.

Thinking through this whole family experience has made me feel less attached to places and things, and more invested in experiencing being with people I love. Mulan will never be younger than she is right now, and neither will I, and neither will Michael. This house will have other families living in it, long after all of us are gone.

I feel I am in the grip of something I helped create, but which now owns me. I remade my world by assembling this family, and now this family has remade me.

My brother Jim said it most bluntly many years ago. He called me, exasperated, when his twins were about four years old. He said, "Julia, I was hoodwinked! The girls are so hard, they are trying to kill each other every minute, they need so much. Tammy and I are at the end of our rope. Everyone said this was going to be so meaningful and fun and that is utter bullshit. It's misery. And yet, I really, really, really love them so much. Which means I am totally and royally screwed!"

When I became a mother, I had no idea that my concern for my own child's welfare would make me a lifetime hostage to fate. But now I am and what can I do? I have to just ride the wave that I have agreed to surf on. It's come at much higher costs than I ever thought, but it has deep rewards.

Mulan recently asked me if I thought her biological mother was alive. I said she probably was. I told Mulan, "I think about her every day." It's true. I wonder about this woman who gave me this fantastic kid. I wish she knew her daughter was thriving. I feel sad that she doesn't get to see her beautiful child's face, which probably looks much like her own.

Mulan said, "I don't think about her that much. Maybe once a month." I loved her candor. Someday Michael, Mulan, and I will go back to China and see the neighborhood in which Mulan was found. When I think of that, I think of us as such a small random unit, passing through this life together in a big, unforgiving, frightening, unpredictable, beautiful, luxurious, breathy world.

Acknowledgments

To Michael Blum, my husband, the best band of hus for me.

To Erin Malone, literary agent extraordinaire.

To Trish Todd, the superwoman editor, who swept in and carried me off in a time of need.

To Paul Haas, agent of my dreams (none of them nightmares).

To Peter Nelson and Mark Wetzstein, not only lawyers, friends, too.

To Norma Blum, a mother-in-law match made in heaven.

To Joel Blum, a god, who pointed his finger and started a new world.

To Aunt Bonnie, who's always there to nudge me in the right direction, where would I be without you?

To Jim, lovely, lucky Jim, my last remaining brother.

To Jim Emerson, my first editor of these pieces, my dear friend, my heart.

To Gino Salomone, my true secret bearer, my deepest laugh sharer.

To Aunt Shirley, who keeps me giggling, and lets me know what pure kind interest feels like

To Pam Kasper, the most wonderful associate/assistant/writing dominatrix imaginable.

To Annie Morse, loving, lovely, wise Annie, very helpful second editor of these stories.

To Meg, my dearest sister.

Acknowledgments

To Nick and Katie and Kaitlyn and Megan Sweeney, my excellent nephew and nieces.

To Richard T. Jameson and Kathleen Murphy, for those times when I needed a sounding board most, my favorite comrades in the art of watching.

To Jill Sobule, who got me to tell many of these stories on stage during our *Jill & Julia Show*.

To Jake Samuels, at Space in Evanston, for allowing me to workshop some of these stories in that most lovely of performance spaces.

To Mary Connors, who helps me figure it all out.

To John Steingart and Jenny Weiner of Ars Nova Theater, thank you for mounting *In the Family Way* and encouraging me to recount many of the stories that I reconfigure in this book.

To Mark Brokaw, the director of *In the Family Way*, what a delightful collaboration.

To Chris Anderson and June Cohen of TED, who gave me the chance to tell my stories several times at the TED conference. TED! The mother of all conferences, and when I say "mother" I mean that in only the best possible way.

A NOTE ON THE AUTHOR

Julia Sweeney was a cast member of *Saturday Night Live* from 1990 to 1994. She has also written and performed in several successful, critically acclaimed one-woman shows, including *God Said, "Ha!"*, which played on Broadway and was made into a film produced by Quentin Tarantino, and *Letting Go of God*, which was performed off-Broadway and was also made into a film. She lives outside of Chicago, Illinois.

@juliasweeney

http://juliasweeney.blogspot.com

A NOTE ON THE TYPE

The text of this book is set in Adobe Garamond. It is one of several
versions of Garamond based on the designs of Claude Garamond.
It is thought that Garamond based his font on Bembo, cut in 1495
by Francesco Griffo in collaboration with the Italian printer Aldus
Manutius. Garamond types were first used in books printed in
Paris around 1532. Many of the present-day versions of this type are
based on the *Typi Academiae* of Jean Jannon cut in Sedan in 1615.